T0339558

Cambridge Elements ≡

Elements in the Politics of Development
edited by
Rachel Beatty Riedl
Einaudi Center for International Studies and Cornell University
Ben Ross Schneider
Massachusetts Institute of Technology

Mario Einaudi
CENTER FOR
INTERNATIONAL STUDIES

 MIT CENTER FOR INTERNATIONAL STUDIES

POWER AND CONVICTION

The Political Economy of Missionary Work in Colonial-Era Africa

Frank-Borge Wietzke
Institut Barcelona d'Estudis Internacionals

 CAMBRIDGE
UNIVERSITY PRESS

CAMBRIDGE
UNIVERSITY PRESS

Shaftesbury Road, Cambridge CB2 8EA, United Kingdom

One Liberty Plaza, 20th Floor, New York, NY 10006, USA

477 Williamstown Road, Port Melbourne, VIC 3207, Australia

314–321, 3rd Floor, Plot 3, Splendor Forum, Jasola District Centre,
New Delhi – 110025, India

103 Penang Road, #05–06/07, Visioncrest Commercial, Singapore 238467

Cambridge University Press is part of Cambridge University Press & Assessment,
a department of the University of Cambridge.

We share the University's mission to contribute to society through the pursuit of
education, learning and research at the highest international levels of excellence.

www.cambridge.org
Information on this title: www.cambridge.org/9781108987172

DOI: 10.1017/9781108982672

First published 2023

A catalogue record for this publication is available from the British Library.

ISBN 978-1-108-98717-2 Paperback
ISSN 2515-1584 (online)
ISSN 2515-1576 (print)

Additional resources for this publication at www.cambridge.org/wietzke.

Power and Conviction

The Political Economy of Missionary Work in Colonial-Era Africa

Elements in the Politics of Development

DOI: 10.1017/9781108982672
First published online: February 2023

Frank-Borge Wietzke
Institut Barcelona d'Estudis Internacionals
Author for correspondence: Frank-Borge Wietzke, fbwietzke@ibei.org

Abstract: This Element engages with recent attempts by economists and political scientists to rigorously estimate impacts of missionary work in sub-Saharan Africa. It argues that, although these efforts contribute to more accurate assessments of the "true" effects of missionary presence, they also have a tendency to present Christian involvement in the region as a largely apolitical process, that was relatively unaffected by the rapidly evolving geopolitical and sociocultural contexts of the colonial period. Countering this trend, this Element illustrates aspects of missionary behavior that were inherently more political and context-dependent, such as local struggles for religious hegemony between Protestants and Catholics and interactions between colonial regimes and the church-based provision of goods like education. The Element draws heavily on market-based theories of organized religious behavior. These perspectives are entirely compatible with the analytical language of economists and political scientists. Yet, they played surprisingly limited roles in recent literature on missionary impacts.

Keywords: Christian missionaries, colonialism, Africa, education, long-run development, politics of religion

ISBNs: 9781108987172 (PB), 9781108982672 (OC)
ISSNs: 2515-1584 (online), 2515-1576 (print)

Contents

An Online Appendix is available at
www.cambridge.org/wietzke.

1 Introduction

The literature on Christian missionary work in colonial-era Africa has gone through multiple turns and phases. Initially dominated by the writing of (mostly white) missionaries, it started with a more self-congratulatory tone – praising rather than questioning the efforts of foreign churches in the region (for overviews see De Haas and Frankema 2018; Porter 2004). This was followed by a period of more critical examination, both within the missionary movement itself and by outside observers. On the ground in Africa and in former metropolitan centers, researchers began to acknowledge the often patronizing – if not openly racist – attitudes of white missionaries, as well as their close involvement in the imposition of colonial rule over the continent (Comaroff and Comaroff 2021; Opoku 1985; Strayer 1976). Missionaries now variably came to be seen as "workhorses of empire" (Abernethey 2000, 226), "partners in hegemony" (Young 1994, 159), or at least as "direct beneficiaries of imperial protection" (Osterhammel 2014, 891).

A more recent, strongly interdisciplinary literature takes the entanglement between missionaries and colonialism largely as a given. However, it pays more attention to how missionaries impacted the long-run development of African societies. Dominated by the work of economists, political scientists, and economic historians, this scholarship tends to treat missionaries as a transformative influence that changed outcomes in areas ranging from education (Alesina et al. 2021; Cage and Rueda 2016; Cogneau and Moradi 2014; Gallego and Woodberry 2010; Meier zu Selhausen and Weisdorf 2016; Montgomery 2017; Nunn 2014; Wantchekon et al. 2015; Wietzke 2014, 2015; Woodberry 2004), to religious beliefs (Nunn 2010), and secondary outcomes, like economic development (Bolt and Bezemer 2009; Grier 1997; Jedwab et al. 2022), and the strength of political institutions (Cage and Rueda 2016; Wantchekon et al. 2015; Woodberry 2004, 2012). A further important innovation in this literature is the use of rigorous quantitative methods and research designs to ensure that observed outcomes are really attributable to missionary work and not other potential confounding factors. Many studies control carefully for influences like local geography, colonial contexts, and preexisting Indigenous institutions (Jedwab et al. 2022; Nunn 2010). Others rely on more sophisticated techniques of causal identification, such as cross border comparisons (Caicedo 2018; Cogneau and Moradi 2014; Dupraz 2019), matching strategies (Cage and Rueda 2016), and instrumental variable regressions (Waldinger 2017; Wietzke 2015; Woodberry 2012).

This Element is favorable to these efforts to carefully isolate and quantify the impacts of missionary interventions.[1] However, it argues that, in trying to

---

[1] My own earlier research also falls into this field. It explored consequences of missionary presence on educational and economic outcomes in Madagascar (see Wietzke 2014, 2015).

establish church-based activities as a process that had independent effects on Africa's long-run development, recent scholarship has sometimes gone too far in downplaying the complex interconnections between missionary work and the wider dynamics of Western political and cultural imperialism in the region. In most of the studies cited above, authors are content to demonstrate that, once colonial and other relevant historical influences are properly "controlled for," Christian proselytizing and service provision had meaningful and statistically discernable impacts on the long-run trajectories of local communities (if not entire countries). By contrast, there has been less attention to the specific ways in which missionary work itself was shaped by the wider social, religious, and geopolitical environment at the eve of the colonial period.

The primary aim of this Element is to bring these historical influences back into the picture. At the basis of my argument is the recognition that attention to history is particularly important in the context of early colonial-era Africa. The reason is that it led to dynamics that differed in distinct ways from experiences with missionary work in other world regions. For instance, in contrast to colonial Latin America – where Christianization was mostly a Catholic affair – large parts of the missionary effort south of the Sahara occurred against the background of often-intense Protestant-Catholic rivalries that had emerged in metropolitan societies since the period of Reformation. On the ground, this led to a veritable "religious scramble" for Africa, as missions of competing denominations struggled to implant their respective interpretation of the Christian faith among the local population (Gallego and Woodberry 2010; Hastings 1996; Pfisterer 1933).[2] I argue in this Element that these competitive behaviors had implications for a range of outcomes, such as the local intensity of proselytizing activity and the organizational and strategic choices adopted by rival missions once they arrived in the region.

Another distinctive factor was the relatively late and uneven onset of colonialism in Africa. For example, in another marked difference to Latin America (and also partly Asia), missionary and colonial forays in the region did not always go hand in hand. In particular further inland, missionaries often arrived decades before colonial states (Hastings 1996; Johnson 1967; Sundkler and Steed 2000). This provided them with the opportunity to pursue their version of the scramble for Africa in a relatively unconstrained manner. Also later, the gradual and highly uneven implantation of colonial rule south of the Sahara meant that, after the continent's partitioning, the degree of institutional variation remained substantial (Herbst 2000; Osterhammel 2014). Once different and

---

[2] Following the literature reviewed here, I focus mostly on missionary activity in the nineteenth and early twentieth century. Earlier Christian influences in the region, as well as competition with other religions like Islam, are discussed in Section 2.

competing colonial powers began asserting their political and regulatory control over the region, missionaries increasingly found themselves in a patchwork of intense nationalist rivalries and evolving regimes that granted varying degrees of protection to "favored" and "non-favored" mission societies (Gallego and Woodberry 2010; Johnson 1967). Again, these contextual influences had important effects on the ambitions, behaviors, and strategic responses of church-based actors on the ground that merit much closer attention.

My theoretical framework analyzes the overlapping missionary and colonial scrambles for Africa under the perspective of market-based models of organized religious behavior. These latter approaches draw on the work of influential thinkers like the sociologist Peter Berger (1969), the economist Laurence Iannaccone (1991), and even Adam Smith (see Section 4). Yet, while they spawned large interdisciplinary literatures about the actions of contemporary faith-based actors in developed and developing regions (Barro and McCleary 2005; Finke and Stark 1988; Trejo 2009; Warner 1993), they have been surprisingly absent from the recent scholarship about missionary work (for notable exceptions see Amasyali 2022; Gallego and Woodberry 2010; Lankina and Getachew 2013). Although I acknowledge that the metaphor of a religious market is itself harder to transplant into an essentially precapitalist environment like Africa before and during the partitioning, I argue that these theories are particularly useful for explaining competitive behaviors of religious organizations in contexts where no single faith system had (yet) established a monopoly over the local population. In particular, outside of traditionally Muslim and Christian regions, the fluidity of religious allegiances and relative absence of states that could enforce monopolies led to particularly high levels of competition that are required for market theory to work.[3]

In addition, the market metaphor allows incorporating growing colonial influences once Western rule became more pervasive. As with other social and economic fields, missionary work under colonialism was shaped in important ways by the regulations and institutional frameworks introduced by the new secular authorities. This mattered in particular in the light of uneven levels of protection that some colonial powers like France, Portugal, and sixteenth- to eighteenth-century in political and institutional environments not only affected

---

[3] This is not to say that Indigenous states and religious authorities that could have enforced monopolies were not present. Key examples were the continent's more advanced Islamic Caliphates and Christian states in Ethiopia or regions that had already come under Catholic influence during the period of Portuguese colonialization. However, in particular societies practicing traditional non-monotheistic religions were often more open to incorporating or at least tolerating the new faith. See Sections 2 and 4 for a more extended discussion.

the intensity of religious competition permitted in different parts of Africa. It also provided favored missions with opportunities to leverage colonial regulations in their struggle for local religious predominance (Gallego and Woodberry 2010).

The empirical sections of this Element set out to illustrate that the proposed change in perspective both matters for the new interdisciplinary literature on missionary impacts, and that it can be relatively easily incorporated into its predominantly quantitative research designs. The first of these examples addresses the question of the geographic distribution of missionary work in Africa. This spatial dimension in the organization of proselytizing and educational activities is one of the most hotly debated topics among those seeking to rigorously evaluate the impacts of missionary interventions. The reason is that systematic imbalances in the distribution of missionary presence may introduce unwanted biases into the analysis. In particular, in cases where missionaries congregated in areas that offered more favorable geographic or socioeconomic conditions, the resulting initial advantages need to be accounted for, before observed differences in the long-run development of these regions can be attributed to missionary activities. Much of the attention in recent quantitative scholarship has thus been devoted to carefully separating out the effects of these confounding factors (see e.g. Cage and Rueda 2016; Jedwab et al. 2022; Nunn 2010).

In Section 5, I introduce Protestants' and Catholics' competition for prospective converts as an additional, hitherto underappreciated, influence on the geographic distribution of missionary work. Using the same historical data sources as many of the quantitative studies cited, I show econometrically that the presence of rival missions and their interactions with colonial regime contexts are a strong predictor for the creation of new mission stations in the early twentieth century. These effects often dominate statistically over those of other more widely studied geographic and socioeconomic determinants of mission placement, such as a region's accessibility, population sizes, or the local disease environment. Moreover, the clustering of missionary activity that is due to religious competition often interacts in unexpected ways with other geography-induced sources of bias in the estimation of missionaries' long-term impacts. In my analysis, higher levels of missionary competition are associated with lower long-run development. This underscores that the consequences of inter-religious rivalry should be considered as an independent factor in attempts to arrive at more reliable assessments of the developmental legacies of missionaries in Africa.

The second example extends the metaphor of a religious market to the more widely studied field of missionary education. The starting point of my discussion is a tendency in recent scholarship to attribute differences in missionary behaviors in this area primarily to diverging norms and doctrinal positions that are *internal* to the major Christian denominations active in Africa. A key example is the Protestant conviction that also lay persons should be able to read the Bible, which has been linked to higher educational investments in former Protestant areas (Becker and Woessmann 2009; Michalopoulos and Papaioannou 2020; Montgomery 2017; Nunn 2014). My use of market theory leads me to de-emphasize these doctrinal positions and to highlight instead *external* influences linked to local religious competition. Without denying that internal norms and values mattered, I argue that, whenever there were higher levels of religious rivalry, other Christian denominations like Catholics also had strong incentives to invest in education in order to attract new converts (see also Gallego and Woodberry 2010; Lankina and Getachew 2013).

The empirical analysis that I present to test this argument introduces an explicitly comparitivist perspective that incorporates variation in the degree of competition that was permitted by different colonial regimes in the field of missionary education. Building on earlier work by Gallego and Woodberry (2010), I argue that in particular British authorities often allowed greater rivalry between missionaries of the major denominations around the provision of religious schooling. This was in contrast to former Francophone, Portuguese, and German territories, where education was both more regulated, and where Catholics in particular often enjoyed comparatively stronger levels of protection from secular powers. Econometric analysis suggests that these contextual factors led to important differences in the strategies adopted by Catholics and Protestants in specific areas of education like female schooling. I show that, while gender-based differences in school attainments are not visible in former Catholic mission districts in the historically more competitive educational markets of British colonies, women in Catholic regions are more likely to trail behind men in the previously more tightly regulated educational systems of French, Portuguese, and German territories. Again, these results support the claim that the work of missionaries did not unfold in a vacuum. Their strategies and behaviors were profoundly shaped by institutional and political environments.

My arguments make several contributions to the emerging new literature about missionary impacts in Africa. First, by incorporating the role of colonial regime environments, this Element expands on earlier research designs that were mostly limited to demonstrating effects of missionary presence in a more generic manner. The comparative perspective used here adds more nuance and structure to these analyses, by documenting that the transformative consequences of different missionary denominations varied in significant and generalizable ways across relevant contexts and institutional settings. In doing so, this work contributes to a small but expanding literature about variation in colonial education systems in Africa (see e.g. Baten et al. 2021; Cogneau and Moradi 2014; Dupraz 2019; Feldmann 2016; White 1996). However, whereas these latter contributions usually only consider faith-based schooling as one of many factors in total education supply, I develop an analytical framework that applies specifically to the work of missionaries. In addition, my analysis extends the discussion beyond the better-studied domain of religious education, to also address important prior processes, such as missionaries' decisions when and where to open new fields for proselytizing activity (Section 5).

Second, this Element moves away from treating missionary work as a relatively neutral "supply shock" that was only determined by practical considerations or doctrinal positions within the major mission churches. In my analysis, missionaries' own hegemonic ambitions in Africa emerge as an important additional factor shaping social, spatial, and even political relations in the region. This emphasis on the political dimensions of missionary work is particularly important in the African context, where the weak implantation of modern states has always led researchers to look beyond the domain of government and formal institutions to explain variation in local socioeconomic and political outcomes (Easton 1959; Fortes and Evans-Pritchard 1940; Herbst 2000; Lloyd 1965). Nonetheless, while earlier scholarship typically focused on "traditional" or "customary" authorities that originated within African societies (e.g. tribes, lineage systems), my focus on Western missionaries shifts the attention to a group of external actors with much closer ties to colonial powers. This approach aligns with other recent attempts to highlight "softer" symbolic and societal dimensions of European rule, that operated below the level of open state coercion and violence (Comaroff and Comaroff 2021; Landau 1995).

Finally, this Element aims to set the stage for a stronger reconnection between the recent, more quantitative literature on mission impacts and the mostly qualitative historiographical scholarship that preceded it. By moving away from treating missionary work as a relatively well-contained, independent influence on African societies, my analysis makes it easier to account for the complex interactions between Western mainline churches and colonialism that constituted a central concern to earlier scholarship in the field of mission studies (see e.g. Groves 1969; Hastings 1996; Porter 2004; Stanley 1990; Strayer 1976; Sundkler and Steed 2000). I hope that further research along the lines outlined in this Element will help reintroduce these latter perspectives, thus unlocking the full potential of the vast interdisciplinary literature on missionary work that emerged over the last one-and-a-half centuries.

The Element proceeds as follows. The next two sections set the stage for my discussion, respectively by outlining the historical context of the period of missionary work considered here (Section 2) and the content and shortcomings of the recent interdisciplinary literature on missionary impacts (Section 3). Section 4 introduces the theory of a religious market and discusses the particular areas of applicability of this perspective in the African context. Section 5 explores the impacts of religious competition on the geographic distribution of mission activity in the region. Section 6 applies the religious market metaphor to the field of religious education. The last section concludes and outlines directions for further research.

2 Historical Context

I begin by outlining the historical context of the period of missionary work covered in this Element. Following the recent interdisciplinary literature reviewed here, I focus mostly on conversionary efforts between the late eighteenth and the early twentieth century. There were, however, several earlier Christian forays into Africa that should also briefly be acknowledged.

The first wave of Christian influences in the region dates back to the days of the first apostles and took place mostly in Egypt, North Africa, Nubia, and Ethiopia. It continued via missionary efforts and migration out of Judea and later Rome through the first four centuries AD (Hastings 1996, 62ff; Sundkler and Steed 2000). However, with the notable exception of Ethiopia, it rarely left an imprint south of the Sahara. It was subsequently interrupted by the rise of Islam from the seventh century onward. Only Ethiopia and a few scattered Christian colonies in North Africa remained firmly Christian (Opoku 1985, 512). Because of this more limited geographic reach and durability, it neither plays a strong role in the literature reviewed here, nor in my own analysis.

The next notable wave of Christian expansion occurred during the early Portuguese colonization of Africa. It was dominated by Capuchin and especially Jesuit priests, who arrived in the continent from the sixteenth century onward. In organizational terms, it closely resembled other episodes of Catholic missionary work in regions like Latin America. Jesuit priests worked under the joint patronage and protection of Pope Alexander IV (1431–1503) and the Portuguese King John III "the Pious" (1502–57). On the ground likewise, relations between missionaries and the state were strong. Most proselytizing activities remained in close vicinity to Portuguese settlements and military outposts (Mkenda 2016; Sundkler and Steed 2000).

Yet, also these efforts did not leave a very durable imprint on the wider African region. While a few self-sustaining pockets of Christianity persisted in regions like present-day Angola and the coastal areas of the Congo (Thornton 1998), foreign mission presence was largely disrupted by the demise of the

Portuguese Empire and the rise of anticlerical attitudes in Europe after the French revolution. The expulsion of Jesuits from the Iberian peninsula and the overseas dominions of Portugal dealt a final blow to this interval of foreign missionary presence in Africa (Mkenda 2016; Pawliková-Vilhanová 2007).

The phase of missionary activity that is the primary focus of this Element, originated in the evangelical revival movement of the late eighteenth century. Its onset is often dated to William Carey's 1792 sermon "Enquiry into the Obligations of Christians to use means for the Conversion of the Heathens." In it, Carey made the case for renewed evangelization efforts in non-Western regions like Africa. The Baptist Missionary Society was founded the same year, followed by the interdenominational London Missionary Society (LMS) in 1795, the evangelical Church Missionary Society (CMS) in 1799, and the British and Foreign Bible Society in 1804. Proselytizing fervor soon also spilled over into other countries, with important missionary organizations emerging in North America and continental Europe, including in France, Germany, Norway, and Switzerland. Although work on the ground in Africa was usually off to a slow start, most of the above organizations established a meaningful foothold in the continent by the middle of the nineteenth century (Hastings 1996; Porter 2004).

The nineteenth-century missionary revival stands out from the aforementioned periods of Portuguese-led Christianization campaigns in Africa and Latin America because of its more uneven relations with secular forms of colonialism. Back at home, in metropolitan centers, the connections were certainly strong. For instance, the timing of William Carey's 1792 sermon broadly coincided with Britain's defeat in the American war of independence in 1783 and the following reorientation of the empire's colonial ambitions to Asia, the Pacific, and Africa. German mission societies likewise were usually created with the explicit intention of delivering education and Christianity to the country's newly acquired colonies (Groves 1969; Johnson 1967). In many German-controlled parts of Asia and the Pacific, missionaries arrived at the same time or even after the colonizers.

By contrast, in Africa, colonialism unfolded too slowly to allow for a close alignment with early missionary efforts. Two broad periods stand out, each with distinctly different levels of mission-state interactions. The first begins with the early nineteenth-century forays of Evangelical and Protestant missions and roughly ends with the more systematic annexation of the African landmass after the continent's partitioning at the 1885 and 1895 Berlin and Brussels conferences. During this period, Christian missions enjoyed a comparatively strong degree of autonomy from the state, as colonial activities were still mostly limited to isolated coastal trading posts and European settlements

(Herbst 2000).[4] While missionaries regularly relied on colonial infrastructures for transport or protection, much of their work took place "far beyond the borders of any colony and undefended by colonial power" (Hastings 1996, 257; see also Ajayi 1965; Ayandele 1966; Boahen 1989). Particularly vivid examples are the journeys of mission pioneers like David Livingston or George Grenfell. Both doubled as missionaries and explorers in the interior of central and southern Africa, long before the arrival of colonial states (Johnson 1967; Sundkler and Steed 2000). Historical cartographic sources also illustrate the relatively strong levels of missionary activity in these regions. Figure 1 reports the location of larger foreign mission stations, combining data from historical atlases by Harlan Beach and William R.M. Roome for 1903 and 1924, respectively.[5] While this captures the situation after the partitioning, the map reveals a considerable mission presence far away from the African coastline, where colonial states only arrived relatively late. The map is overlaid here with the location of European explorer routes and early twentieth-century railway lines to further illustrate the close but also incomplete connection between early missionary work and the first European forays into Africa.

Catholic missionary activity likewise underwent a significant revival during the nineteenth century. The combined experiences of the (earlier) expansion of Islam and later Protestantism left leading Catholic clergy with the impression that the Holy Roman Church was falling behind in a region that was long considered as its natural sphere of influence. Although Catholic missionary efforts took time to recover from their hiatus described above, the Catholic Church's return to Africa typically trailed the arrival of its Protestant rivals only by few decades. In the Nile region and the continent's Northeast, renewed missionary efforts were initially spearheaded by Italian priests of the Verona Fathers. In Western, Central, and Southern Africa, it started mostly as a French initiative. Leading organizations included the White Fathers (named for the color of their dress, not their skin), who operated out of Algiers, the Congregation of the Holy Ghost, and the Society of African Missions (SMA). Portuguese, Belgian, and German Catholics also (re)turned to the continent in large numbers, following the rise in colonial ambitions in their home countries (Mkenda 2016; Pawliková-Vilhanová 2007).

The second period of missionary activity covered in this Element went along with much stronger state-church interactions. Nominally, it began with the

---

[4] The primary exceptions were the early settler colonies of southern Africa, the Maghreb, and the Senegambia. Here colonial and missionary activity already overlapped more strongly in the nineteenth century (Sundkler and Steed 2000).

[5] These maps were digitized by Cage and Rueda (2016) and Nunn (2010) respectively. See Section 3 for a longer discussion.

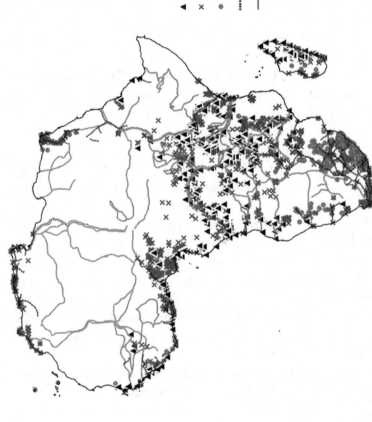

Figure 1 Distribution of missions in Africa.

Source: Author's calculations based on data from Roome (1925) and Beach (1903). These sources were digitized and made available by Nunn (2010) and Cage and Rueda (2016), respectively. Data on railway lines and explorer routes are also from Nunn (2010)

- ▲ Catholic Mission (Roome, 1924)
- ✕ Protestant Mission (Roome, 1924)
- ● Protestant Mission (Beach, 1903)
- ⋯⋯ Railway line (1911)
- —— Explorer Route

colonial partitioning of Africa at the 1885 Berlin and 1890 Brussels conferences. However, in reality, its onset was more gradual, as it usually took time for colonial powers to establish control over the territories awarded to them (Herbst 2000; Pierskalla et al. 2019).

Colonial influences around this time shaped missionary work in multiple ways. The closing documents of the Berlin and Brussels conferences contained relatively strong stipulations to protect the freedom and mobility of missionaries of all denominations (see Section 4). However, the implementation of these commitments was uneven across colonial territories. For instance, European powers like Belgium, France, Germany, Italy, and Portugal generally preferred missionaries from their own societies and often supported them through subsidies or regulatory measures (Johnson 1967; Woodberry 2004; Zorn 2012). This introduced important variations in the opportunities and behaviors of "favored" and "non-favored" missionaries across colonies in Africa (Gallego and Woodberry 2010).

Colonial regimes also soon began to play a stronger role in the important area of missionary education. Countries like France, Portugal, and Belgium again often advantaged missionaries from their home countries, such as by introducing comparatively tight licensing requirements for mission school teachers or by demanding that instruction happened in the language of the colonizers. The British famously took a relatively more hands-off approach, allowing missionaries of all backgrounds and denominations to provide education to the local populace (Clignet and Foster 1964; White 1996). A good part of this Element will be devoted to analyzing how these differences in colonial policies shaped behaviors in this particularly important domain of missionary activity.

2.1 Ideological Overlaps between Missionaries and Colonizers

The varying interactions between missionaries and colonizers are of sufficient importance for this Element's overall argument to merit more detailed discussion. In the following sections, I address this need by substantiating my claim that missionary and colonial forays in the region really represented two interrelated but also partially independent "scrambles for Africa." I begin by discussing the shared ideological premises that connected both of these scrambles. I then discuss emerging areas of disagreement that erupted primarily over the role that the church was to play in colonial societies. On the side of missionary movement, this was grounded in an often deep-seated religiosity that also provided the foundations for the missionary part of the scramble.

The main glue that initially held together the missionary and colonial scrambles was the belief that Western societies had a fundamental right (if not obligation) to bring their "superior" culture and civilization to Africa. To leading missionaries in the early and mid-nineteenth century, Christianization was but one pillar in their wider efforts of cultural and economic transformation of African peoples. This conviction is well expressed in the famous "three C's" (Christianity, Civilization, and Commerce), often attributed to David Livingstone, but also widely used by other missionaries and statesmen at the time (Hastings 1996, 282ff). According to many nineteenth-century missionaries, Christianity not only furnished "a complete moral machinery for carrying forward all the great processes which lie at the root of civilization." It also brought the "heathens" the prospect of "unlimited social and economic development" (Stanley 1983, 71, citing the missionary W. Ellis).

A particularly good example for these overlaps was the humanitarian movement that developed in metropolitan centers around the issue of slavery. Back at home, in the elite circles of cities like London, Washington, and New York, leading representatives of the church collaborated closely with members of government, senior military, and public intellectuals to lobby for the adoption of abolitionist policies (Groves 1969; Porter 2004). Also on the ground in Africa, missionaries concurred with more transformative elements within colonial regimes in that they saw the introduction of modern forms of production and commerce as the best way out of the region's traditional slave-based economies. In particular early Protestant efforts were often devoted to establishing alternative forms of income and commerce, such as by opening model farms or training local converts in crafts like tailoring, printing, or carpentry (Boahen 1989; Groves 1969; Hastings 1996; Pawliková-Vilhanová 2007). In Western Africa, but also parts of the continent's eastern and southern regions, these interventions provided critical foundations for the emergence of modern colonial economies and the shift to "legitimate" goods like palm oil and groundnuts (Austin 2004; Githige 1982; Pawliková-Vilhanová 2007).

Other contributions to the colonial project were of a more indirect nature, through the transfer of Western beliefs and institutions. Postcolonialism scholars have long argued that racially infused role models and identities promoted by white missionaries helped stabilize colonial regimes. A well-known example is the work of the anthropologists Jean and John Comaroff, who made this case forcefully for present-day South Africa. They posit that, while seemingly only concerned with purely "religious" questions, missionaries profoundly influenced status relations, identities, and everyday practices in ways that often prepared Africans to be "docile laborers at the bottom end of the emerging capitalist economy and docile citizens in the newly forming states" (Comaroff and Comaroff 2021, 447; see also Comaroff and Comaroff 1993; Frederiks and Nagy 2021).

Finally, in more material terms, core mission activities like the provision of education and other social services created important underpinnings for colonial states and economies. For instance, missionary school curricula may have prioritized religious content, but they also provided skills and education that prepared Africans for work in colonial administrations and the modern business sector (Berman 1974; Boahen 1989; Leach 2008; Wallerstein 1961). Also more generally, missionary provision of health and education helped ease the worst distortions of colonialism, while the involvement of local communities in the delivery of these services laid the foundations of future civil society and voluntary sectors that took forward the task of social development in the postindependence period (Jennings 2013; Woodberry 2012).

How did missionaries deal with the fervent nationalisms and geopolitical rivalries that underpinned the colonial scramble for Africa? Most were men and women of their time who struggled to free themselves from the strong patriotic currents that ran through their home societies. This was particularly apparent among Protestants and Catholics from Germany, whose mission organizations were usually created with the explicit objective of delivering Christianity and literacy to the country's newly acquired colonies (Groves 1969; Hastings 1996). However, also in France, early Catholic missionary efforts had strong national ties (Sundkler and Steed 2000, 100ff). For instance, Hastings (1996, 255) describes the head and founder of the French Catholic White Fathers – Cardinal Lavigerie – as "very much a French statesman" who regarded the French conquest of Africa as "a matter of high pride." Even in supposedly more secular societies like Britain, missionaries often had few inhibitions to associate themselves with their government. A well-known example is again provided by David Livingstone, who readily accepted the title of British Consul and subsequently completed some of his African journeys under this mandate (Roberts 2008).

Those missionaries who took a more independent stand similarly believed that, if there had to be colonization, it should at least come from their own homelands. Many hoped that the interests and accomplishments of their respective church would be better protected from encroachments by "foreign" rivals, if political control was exercised by their fellow countrymen (Beidelman 1974; Groves 1969; Opoku 1985, 513). A widely referenced – albeit extreme – case was the behavior of the CMS during a long-brewing conflict between competing Protestant and Catholic factions in late nineteenth-century Buganda. Leading CMS missionaries actively lobbied for the annexation of the region by the Imperial British East Africa Company and even raised money to ensure that its forces stayed on after the company had run out of funds. A Catholic victory was believed to have disastrous consequences for the local prospects of

Protestantism and thus had to be avoided at all cost. The collaboration resulted in the defeat of previously ascendant pro-Catholic forces in the battle of Mengo in 1892, following the intervention of Captain Frederick Lugard and his Maxim machine guns (De Haas and Frankema 2018; Hastings 1996, 411f).

2.2 Areas of Disagreement

Despite the above alignments, it is important not to overstate the actual degree of overlap between missionary and colonial ambitions. On the one hand, there was the well-documented resistance against colonial abuses that is often highlighted in literature about the politically modernizing legacies of missionary presence (Groves 1969; Woodberry 2004, 2012). Although many missionaries were convinced of the "natural right" of Westerners to rule and "civilize" Africans, they also believed that power bore moral responsibility. This sentiment was usually held as a matter of principle and it was further reinforced by the pragmatic consideration that missions would lose Africans' support if they became too closely associated with colonial abuses. Disputes between missionaries, colonial authorities, and settlers arose frequently in these contexts across Africa. A widely noted example is the "Red Rubber" campaign against human rights abuses in the Belgium Congo. It combined documentary evidence collected by missionaries on the ground with lobbying by church-based organizations and publicists in the metropolitan centers of Europe and America (Groves 1969; Murhula 2018). Illustrative cases also exist for other periods and regions, such as the well-documented efforts of the Protestant priest John Philip (1775–1851) to secure basic rights for Africans in the Cape Colony (Groves 1969; Woodberry 2004), and recurrent interventions of leading clergy over land and labor issues in Kenya, Uganda, and Botswana (Githige 1982; Hastings 1996; Woodberry 2011).[6]

Other sources of disagreement were of a more cultural and sociological nature. Qualitative mission historiography indicates that those churchmen and women who came to Africa were often separated from the rest of white colonial and settler society by their profound spiritualism and associated anti-modern attitudes (Beidelman 1974; Leach 2008; Strayer 1976). For many of them, part of the motivation to take up the difficult and frequently life-threatening task of proselytizing in far-away lands was precisely the desire to escape from the "rationalism, materialism, and urbanization" that was eating away at their preferred vision of a Christian civilization back home (Strayer 1976, 12f).

For these more conservatively inclined missionaries, religious motivations often trumped alignments with colonial powers. The case is usually made most forcefully

---

[6] Note however, that missionaries were often implicated in land conflicts themselves, as they too required tribal land for their farms (Githige 1982).

for the evangelical arm of the movement, whose belief in an "all-embracing, superintending Providence" only allowed for a "comparatively insignificant place" for empire (Porter 2004, 58f). However, anti-secular attitudes also existed among other denominations. The historian Markowitz describes Catholic priests in the Congo as deeply anti-modern and "anti-cosmopolitan." He observes that many of them "idealized African village life and rejected such aspects of modernity as urbanization and industrialization" (Markowitz 1973, 13). Similar claims have been made about important Catholic leaders like Cardinal Lavigerie of the White Fathers (Sundkler and Steed 2000, 104ff). Turning to Protestants from Britain and Germany, Hastings (1996) and Beidelman (1974) note that those willing to expose themselves to the arduous realities of life in nineteenth-century Africa, were usually of modest educational background and remained "rather little affected by the more secularizing and critical aspects of late Victorian culture" (Hastings 1996, 253).[7]

The above conservative tendencies within the missionary movement naturally led to profound disagreements with colonial authorities over the types of states and societies to be created in the region. Moreover, the particularities of the wider historical setting of Western imperialism in Africa again mattered in this context. By the time meaningful levels of missionary and colonial presence were established, ruling elites of colonial powers had long been exposed to strong secularizing influences. For conservative missionaries, this often created unacceptable tensions. As the "perils" of secularization and modernization began to become visible also in the colonies, many of them even renounced the "civilizatory" philosophy and openness to commerce that tied together missionary and imperial ambitions during the time of early church pioneers like David Livingstone (Hastings 1996; Pawliková-Vilhanová 2007). The goal became increasingly to protect the deep spiritualism encountered in many African communities and to rebuild "the church of Christ" within this welcoming environment (Strayer 1976, 13). The ideal was "a Christian kingdom of an early medieval type," where the church would play a central in the organization of social and political affairs (Hastings 1996, 429).

2.3 The Scramble within the Scramble

The strength of religious convictions described above also provided the foundations for the missionary scramble for Africa. While it is true that missionaries of all denominations first and foremost wanted to convert as many nonbelievers as possible, it was particularly important that *their* religion and respective interpretation of Christianity would come to dominate the minds and souls of the local population.

---

[7] Beidelman and Hastings both explicitly extend their argument to local staff of wealthier and more scholarly mission organizations like the CMS and the University Mission Society.

The unfolding of the missionary scramble can, again, be divided into two historical processes. The first concerns missionaries' rivalry with Islam. Many of the early mission pioneers arriving to Africa were well aware of the "threat" posed by this other monotheistic religion. Especially in West Africa and the Sahel, Muslim influence had increased steadily as a result of the Fulani Jihads, trade, and the creation of large caliphates like Sokoto and Tukulor (Opoku 1985). Nonetheless, important Muslim communities also existed further east, such as among the Yao and the Baganda and along the Swahili-speaking coast of East Africa. In many of these regions, early missionary activity at least partially reflected the desire to halt, if not reverse the expansion of Islam (Hastings 1996). However, also the strong Christian presence deeper inland, such as in the Congo and central Africa, can be interpreted as an attempt to prevent the further spread of Muslim influences (Johnson 1967; Sundkler and Steed 2000).

The second process, which will receive more attention in this Element, was the rivalry between Catholics and Protestants. To some leading church historians, Protestant-Catholic competition was such a self-evident element of the nineteenth- and twentieth-century missionary push into Africa that it barely necessitates further mention (see e.g. Sundkler and Steed 2000, 294). However, others made it a more central piece of their analysis. For instance, Hastings (1996, 397ff), on whose terminology I draw here, speaks of a "variety of scrambles." Gallego and Woodberry (2010), Mkenda (2018), Murhula (2018), and Pfisterer (1933) also engage in more detail with the nuances and consequences of Protestant-Catholic competition.

As noted, for Catholics in particular it was unfathomable that Africa should gradually be taken over not only by Islam but also by the recent Protestant "upstarts." The continent was considered the natural hinterland of the Catholic Church, which itself could already look back on a proud history in the region. Most leading Catholics dreamed of the "retaking" (French: "reprise") of mission fields lost to other religions (Hastings 1996; Johnson 1967; Sundkler and Steed 2000, 287ff). The earlier demise of their faith in the continent was but a temporal aberration that needed to be rectified. For example, Cardinal Lavigerie of the White Fathers consistently emphasized the legacy of the first churches in the early Christian era and during the time of Portuguese hegemony. As a former Professor of Church History at the Sorbonne, he was well aware of the accomplishments of the ancient Churches in Egypt, Roman Africa, Nubia, and Ethiopia and consistently stressed them in his writings (Pawliková-Vilhanová 2007, 251).[8]

---

[8] His full title was "Archbishop of Algiers and Carthage, Primate of Africa and Apostolic Delegate for the Sahara and the Sudan," which, in itself, reflects the scope of his ambitions.

Francis Xavier Vogt, the German-speaking Bishop of the Holy Ghost Fathers in German East Africa felt "impelled in face of the progress of Islam and the Protestant missions" (F. Vogt, cited in Balthazar and Kieffer 1985, 34). He saw the principal duty of his church "to occupy the country by rural schools in order to close it to Islam and the Protestants" (F. Vogt, cited in Hastings 1996, 421). Catholic legal doctrine, issued through papal encyclicals and apostolic letters, likewise regarded collaboration with Protestants as "in error and deceived"[9] and placed all non-Catholics (non-Christian *and* Christian) under the spiritual care of the Catholic church (Pfisterer 1933, 164f; Sundkler and Steed 2000).[10]

As the pioneers of the early nineteenth-century missionary revival, Protestants in many ways felt less immediate pressure to compete. Indeed, faced with the daunting task of reaching all of the vast and largely unexplored African landmass, cooperation and coordination with missionaries with shared beliefs seemed to offer the more logical solution. Consequently, the early Protestant missionary movement was decidedly cooperative in nature and behavior. For example, in the Anglophone sphere, important missionary organ- izations like the LMS were explicitly conceived as interdenominational entities (Porter 2004). Also more generally, collaboration across organizational and even national boundaries was not at all uncommon. Hastings (1996, 246f) describes the Protestant missionary movement at the time as "a singularly non-denominational function of international Protestantism ... The political leadership of the movement could be English, its personnel German, Scottish, or, a little later, French, Scandinavian, or American. They were united in spreading a non-denominational Protestant gospel" (see also Sundkler and Steed 2000, 112f).

The cooperative nature of Protestant work further became manifest under the "comity" principle. Comity reflected an early missionary brand of ecumenism that required Protestant missions to confine their activities to particular territor- ies (Höschele 2010; Sundkler and Steed 2000, 402f). It was first developed by leading clergy in the field and later formalized by the 1910 Edinburgh World Missionary Conference. By dividing their efforts into mutually recognized territorial spheres of influence, Protestant missions sought to minimize interfer- ence in the work of other groups, while simultaneously saving resources and

---

[9] Papal encyclical *Mortalium animos* issued 1928 by Pius XI (www.vatican.va/content/pius-xi/en/ encyclicals/documents/hf_p-xi_enc_19280106_mortalium-animos.html).

[10] Catholics also knew their share of internal rivalry. See, for example, Ranger (1999) and Sundkler and Steed (2000, 294f) for illustrations from Zimbabwe and the Congo. Nonetheless, this changed with the growing centralization of missionary efforts under the tutelage of the Vatican in the early twentieth century (Section 4).

laying the foundations for the unity of all Protestants in a given country (Hoeschele 2010 and Sundkler and Steed 2000; Latourette 1963).[11]

Yet, also Protestants were no strangers to religious competition. Comity explicitly only applied to their own arm of the missionary movement. Moreover, its cooperative elements also served the purpose of creating a strong, united front against other religions and in particular the Catholic church. For instance, further elaborations at the Kikuyu Conference in 1913 referred explicitly to the (perceived) threat of the rival influences of Catholicism and Islam (Porter 2004, 325). Equally competitive instincts emerge from the correspondence of Protestants on the ground. "Saturate the people with the Word of God and you will stop both Mohammedanism and Roman Catholicism" wrote one representative of the Universities Mission to Central Africa to his Bishop (cited in Hastings 1996, 421). Murhula (2018, 194) outlines how Protestant Baptist missionaries in the Belgian Congo regarded Jesuits as "reaping temporal privileges from the state as imposters posing as religious." Similarly negative views of Catholic missions emerge from Protestant correspondence out of German territories (Pfisterer 1933). Ranger further notes that missionaries of the American Methodists in Rhodesia and Mozambique "believed that they had a divine mission to save Africans ... not only from slavery and paganism but also from Catholic superstition" (Ranger 1999, 176).

Figure 1 earlier in this section provides a good illustration of the consequences of Protestant-Catholic rivalry. Missions of both denominations cluster in the coastal areas of West Africa, as well as in the Congo and in particular in the Great Lakes region around present-day Uganda, Rwanda, and Burundi. In places like precolonial Buganda, relations deteriorated so far as to result in open military conflict, as discussed previously. However, even where violence was avoided, rivalries could be intense. Particularly well-documented examples of antagonistic relations exist for West Africa, the continent's East Coast and Madagascar, the Congo, and down into the southern settler territories (Rabeson 2017; Ranger 1999; Sundkler and Steed 2000). Matters only improved with the broadening of the international ecumenical movement after World War II and around the Second Vatican Council from 1962 onward (see Section 7).

2.4 Outlook –Bringing Colonial Institutions Back In

The missionary part of the scramble will be one of the two primary ingredients for the market-based theory that I will develop in Section 4 of this Element. Colonial contexts and interventions the second. As with any other market-type

---

[11] This did not always work perfectly. For example, overlapping Protestant activities existed in particularly popular missionary fields like Southern Africa (Johnson 1967; Sundkler and Steed 2000, 402f).

system, constraints and incentives faced by the actors operating within it depend critically on the degree of competition permitted by relevant governing authorities. Without denying that such authorities also existed in Africa before the colonial period, it was the gradual and varied onset of Western rule that set the most important boundaries for the extent of competition experienced by missionaries: As outlined above, the relative absence of colonial states and regulations initially allowed for a high degree of autonomy in which competition between various religions and Christian denominations could unfold with only few constraints. Later, after the partitioning, colonial regimes provided much stricter guardrails and regulations. Nonetheless, I argue in Section 4 that also during this period, the core principles of a competitive religious market largely remained intact. In particular treaties like the 1885 and 1890 Berlin and Brussels conference accords included strong commitments to religious freedoms that made it hard for colonial powers to entirely ban unwanted missionary organizations from their territory. What differed was the interpretation of these agreements and the degree of protection offered to favored missionary groups.

The resulting variation in the extent of competition faced by different mission societies should be taken into account in a complete analysis of the manifestations and long-term consequences of the Christian revival in Africa. However, before I develop this case in a more systematic manner, I return first to the recent interdisciplinary literature on mission impacts that provided the original motivation for this Element. I argue that, in their efforts to isolate the effects of missionary presence on long-run development, researchers often overlook the complexity of the interactions between missionary work and colonial contexts. The next section will illustrate these shortcomings by way of a more detailed review of the most important contributions to this new body of scholarship.

3 Ignoring the Obvious? The Limited Attention to Colonial Contexts in the Recent Literature on Mission Impacts

As the sources cited in the previous section illustrate, the work, accomplishments, and internal contradictions of the missionary movement have been the subject of a long-running debate among church historians, Africanists, and ethnographers (see e.g. Ajayi 1965; Ayandele 1966; Hastings 1996; Opoku 1985; Ranger 1986; Strayer 1976; Sundkler and Steed 2000; Wright 1971). By contrast, in other disciplines like political science and economics, missionary work only moved into the focus fairly recently. For example, in the former, it took the dissertation of the then doctoral student Robert Woodberry to alert scholars to the fact that in particular the presence of Protestant missionaries often had measurable effects on the long-run performance of democratic institutions (Woodberry 2004; see also Woodberry 2012). In economics, missionary work began to receive attention after the Harvard Professor Nathan Nunn unearthed and digitized cartographic information about historical Catholic and Protestant missions in order to trace longer-term trends in education and religious conversion rates (Nunn 2010, 2014). Since then, a steadily expanding literature on the scale and consequences of missionary work emerged in both disciplines, as well as in related fields such as economic history and development studies (see e.g. De Haas and Frankema 2018; Frankema 2012; Meier zu Selhausen and Weisdorf 2016; Montgomery 2017; Wietzke 2014, 2015).

In addition to deepening the interdisciplinary nature of research on Christian missionaries, the arrival of these new contributions is of interest because it also introduced important novel analytical perspectives. As proponents of disciplines that usually deal with wider questions of state and societal performance, political scientists and economist are usually more willing than researchers from other fields to single out and study missionaries as a self-standing influence on the long-run trajectories of non-Western regions. Conceptually, these investigations are typically embedded in frameworks that regard missionaries as a bottom-up, societal process that influenced outcomes from outside the legal and political institutions of the state. Moreover, they are usually supported by carefully executed quantitative research designs that seek to disentangle missionary efforts from other confounding factors (see e.g. Cage and Rueda 2016; Nunn 2010; Woodberry 2012).

My intention here is not to argue against these attempts to rigorously isolate and quantify the distinct long-run effects of missionary work. However, I posit that the preoccupation with measuring impacts has often led to a tendency to either downplay or overlook the complex ways in which the missionary scramble for Africa interacted with its relevant historical contexts. The very logic of the recent literature has been to present missionary activity as an *independent* influence on long-run development, *net* of potentially confounding variables. This makes it harder to account for the multiple interdependencies between missionary efforts and the wider social, religious, and geopolitical environments of pre- and early colonial-era Africa that were outlined in the previous section.

To illustrate these concerns, the next paragraphs proceed by outlining some of the foundational publications in the new literature on missionary impacts. I focus in particular on the specific conceptual and methodological reasons that explain why these contributions struggle to incorporate relevant social and geopolitical contexts of missionary work at the dawn of the colonial era. I will also briefly discuss recent critical perspectives that have started to pinpoint previously overlooked analytical and data-related issues that pose challenges for attempts to quantify the effects of missionary work. The overall aim of this section is to outline the current status of debate and to zoom in on the specific gaps in the literature that this Element seeks to address.

3.1 Key Examples from Recent Literature

In the new literature on mission studies, the work of Robert Woodberry represents by far one of the most influential contributions. Woodberry's best-known article "The Missionary Roots of Liberal Democracy" is cited close to 650 times[12] and received six awards since its publication in the *American Political Science Review* (Woodberry 2012; see also Woodberry 2004, 2008). Its main theoretical innovation is to turn conventional modernization theory on its head. Woodberry challenges the claim that democracy developed as a result of secularization and socioeconomic modernization. Instead he argues that, at least in non-Western societies, these processes were in fact triggered by educational interventions and other social transformations that were introduced exogenously by conversionary Protestants (Nikolova and Polansky 2020).

The primary empirical support for Woodberry's arguments comes from cross-country regressions that demonstrate a positive correlation between historical Protestant mission presence and postindependence levels of democracy in 142 non-European societies.[13] While more recent research suggests that these results may be sensitive to the choice of time periods and measures of the dependent variable, the findings survive robustness tests that include Catholics in the indicator for Christian presence (Nikolova and Polansky 2020).[14] Several of Woodberry's key claims are also supported by other cross-country studies that report generally positive associations between Christian presence and long-term development (Bolt and Bezemer 2009; Grier 1997; Porta et al. 1997).

The aforementioned work by Nathan Nunn similarly seeks documenting transformative effects of historical missionary presence. His main methodological innovation is the unearthing and digitization of W. R. M. Roome's 1924 map of mission activity in Africa that was used in Section 2 to create Figure 1. The finer-grained depiction of mission presence makes progress over the cross-national studies by Woodberry and other authors because it also allows analyzing how effects of mission presence varied within countries and colonial territories. Consequently, the map is by now one of the most frequently cited

---

[12] https://scholar.google.com/citations?user=pRq_2ZcAAAAJ.

[13] To demonstrate causality, Woodberry employs instrumental variable regressions and over fifty controls.

[14] These qualifications are consistent with arguments developed in Section 4 that differences between Protestants and Catholics were often less strong than authors like Woodberry suggest.

historical sources on Africa-wide missionary activity in the quantitative literature reviewed here (see e.g. Jedwab et al. 2022; Montgomery 2017; Nunn 2010,
2014; Okoye 2021). In his own work, Nunn uses this data to demonstrate
positive long-run associations between mission presence, Christian conversion
rates and contemporary educational outcomes. Other research that followed
Nunn's often maintains this subnational focus but introduces other Africa-wide
sources or country-specific archival data. Relevant examples include Cage and
Rueda (2016) who report and digitize Harlan Beach's 1903 Atlas of Protestant
missionary activity in Africa that is also used in Figure 1.[15] Cogneau and
Moradi (2014) and Jedwab et al. (2021) present historical church statistics for
the Gold Coast/Ghana, while Montgomery (2017), Okoye (2021), and Wietzke
(2014, 2015) do so for German East Africa, Nigeria, and Madagascar,
respectively.

It is worth highlighting that, except for Jedwab et al. (2021), all of the above
contributions draw on missionary data from the early 1900s – hence a time
when the recent colonial partitioning meant that interactions between missionary and colonial regimes were increasing. This context, as well as the general
connectedness of missionary work and Western imperialism, are generally well
acknowledged by the studies reviewed here. However, as noted, the overall
tendency has been to highlight missionary *in*dependence rather than *inter*-
dependence. In the majority of cases, the aim has been to demonstrate that
missionaries shaped outcomes through channels that were distinct from other
colonial-era institutions. By contrast, there has been comparatively little effort
to document how missionary work *interacted* with political regimes and other
relevant historical contexts.

Woodberry's work again provides a good illustration. For Woodberry,
Protestant missionaries are of interest, primarily because they represented an
alternative influence on non-Western societies that often mitigated or even
offset some of the more negative aspects of colonialism. To justify this claim,
he highlights many of the missionary interventions discussed above in
Section 2, such as Protestants' lobbying against colonial abuses of the native
population, their supply of modern education, the transfer of new technologies
like book-printing, as well as the introduction of (parish-based) organizational
structures and "cultures of voluntarism" that subsequently provided foundations
for modern civil society sectors outside of the state (Woodberry 2004, 2012; see
also Jennings 2013; Lankina and Getachew 2012). Of the authors reviewed
here, Woodberry also comes closest to this Element's theoretical approach by

---

[15] Beach's Atlas also contains information on the equipment and qualitative attributes of mission
stations, which the authors use to document specific impacts of mission printing presses. See
Section 6 for a further use of these data.

stressing the importance of religious competition. Among other arguments, Woodberry posits that especially Protestant school provision often had far-reaching catalyzing effects, by incentivizing other actors like the Catholic Church and secular authorities to also invest in education (Gallego and Woodberry 2010; Woodberry 2012; see also Amasyali 2022).

In methodological terms, however, Woodberry's work tends to downplay the role of historical contexts. In particular, his aforementioned article in the *American Political Science Review* presents a set cross-national "horse race" regressions, where measures of mission presence compete with other colonial-era controls for statistical influence over the dependent variable (contemporary democratic performance). Consistent with Woodberry's expectations, this analysis produces a statistical effect for Protestant missions that dominates over that of other widely used colonial-era predictors of long-run development, such as British legal origin or European settler shares (Woodberry 2004, 2012). Nonetheless, by design, Protestant missions and colonial institutions emerge as entirely *separate* influences in these estimates. By contrast, with the notable exception of other work with Francisco Gallego (2010) discussed in more length below, Woodberry's statistical analyses pay little direct attention to *interactions* between missionary and colonial influences.

Nathan Nunn likewise makes clear that, similar to Woodberry, he regards missionary work as a process that influenced African societies primarily from *outside* the colonial state. By his own account, research on the subject is of interest because it forms part of a broader analytical turn in economics and related disciplines toward the social and cultural foundations of economic and political development (Nunn 2010, 2014; see also Guiso et al. 2006; Helmke and Levitsky 2004; Porta et al. 1997; Putnam 1993). In this view, missionary presence emerges mostly as a societal influence that shaped long-run outcomes from below the formal legal and political institutions of government (Nunn 2010).

Again, this perspective leads to important departures from the approach endorsed in this Element. For one, the emphasis on the cultural dimensions of missionary work means that little attention is paid to the competitive struggles for religious hegemony that existed during the colonial-era Christian revival in Africa. For Nunn, the period is primarily of interest because the presence of multiple Catholic and Protestant denominations permits comparing the effects of different theological beliefs and doctrines on behaviors and long-term development (see also Michalopoulos and Papaioannou 2020; Montgomery 2017; Waldinger 2017). However, there is no consideration of the consequences of the competition that existed between rival faith systems and missionary factions (see also Section 6).

In addition, Nunn's empirical work provides another example of research designs that deliberately separate missionary from colonial influences. As with other contributions cited above, Nunn's continent-wide research based on Roome's mission map accounts for colonial contexts primarily through the inclusion of territory- or country-specific "fixed effects." These binary controls remove any nation- or colony-wide differences in observed averages on the dependent and independent variables. In doing so, they effectively limit the estimation only to variation in local missionary activity *within* countries or colonial territories. The resulting analyses yield more accurate estimates of the localized effects of Catholic and Protestant missions. However, their mode of presentation usually leaves little room for a meaningful discussion of possible interactions between missionary work and colonial regime environments. For instance, in his previously cited articles, Nunn reports localized impacts of Catholic and Protestant presence on Christian conversion rates and long-run educational outcomes as Africa-wide averages, without specific attention to whether these effects are observed in, say, former Francophone, Anglophone, or German colonies. Other aforementioned literature that followed in the wake of Nunn's work also often adopted this format. For example, like Nunn, Cage and Rueada (2016) use continent-wide fixed-effects regressions to document positive average associations between mission printing presses, local literacy rates, newspaper readership, and self-reported political activism. Jedwab et al. (2022) employ similar research designs to analyze the relationship between missionary presence and contemporary economic development.

Yet, even from within the quantitative literature reviewed here, there are indications that this relative inattention to colonial contexts can be an important omission. In one of his earlier publications, Woodberry, together with his co-author Francisco Gallego, develops his claim that competition by Protestant schooling incentivized also Catholic missions to invest in education (Gallego and Woodberry 2010). Their analysis indicates that effects of Protestant-Catholic rivalry were particularly visible in former British colonies, where authorities permitted a relatively high degree of missionary competition in the field of religious education. In the literature discussed here, this work comes closest to my own argument that it is important to study interactions between missionaries' own hegemonic ambitions and colonial regime environments. However, this line of research was not pursued in systematic fashion either in Woodberry's other research or the literature triggered by it.

Other contributions document influences of colonial regimes in the context of wider historical analyses of African education systems. For instance, Cogneau and Moradi (2014) and Dupraz (2019) exploit the partitioning of, respectively, former German Togoland and Cameroon after World War I to evaluate impacts of British and French approaches to schooling. Both studies find higher levels of educational attainment in regions that became British after the redrawing of borders. The authors attribute these results to more favorable attitudes toward missionary schooling in British than in French colonies. Frankema (2012), De Haas and Frankema (2018), and Baten et al. (2021) similarly show that educational attainments tend to be higher and more evenly distributed in former British territories, where missionaries enjoyed greater liberties. Nonetheless, in all of these studies, missionaries merely feature as one of multiple elements of colonial and postcolonial education systems. Additional, more focused analysis of the interaction between missionary behavior and colonial regime contexts is thus still merited.

3.2 Excurse: Other Critical Perspectives

Before I continue with outline of my own theoretical arguments, I briefly discuss other critiques that surfaced at multiple points in the literature on mission studies. The first aligns with my claim that recent research has paid insufficient attention to the interplay between missionary and colonial institutions. As noted in Section 2, leading postcolonialism scholars like Jean and John Comaroff have long highlighted the enabling role played by missionaries in the colonial endeavor. The Comaroffs stress in particular that the social and cultural role models that were transferred by conservative arms of the missionary movement helped cement Africans' subordinate status in colonial societies (Comaroff and Comaroff 1993, 2021; see also Landau 1995; Ranger 1986). Also before these contributions, observers with more critical viewpoints long questioned the various cultural biases and often-anachronistic social norms introduced by white missionaries. Starting in the 1950s, a "nationalist" school of mission studies began exploring in more depth the foreign clergy's complicated entanglement in the colonial endeavor (for overviews see Strayer 1976; Wright 1971). Drawing on analyses of missionary correspondence and archival records, this literature revealed that many white missionaries were no less racist than other Europeans (Hastings 1996; Strayer 1976, 1). Scholarship at the time also moved away from treating missionary work as exclusively driven by European and American efforts. Especially African researchers documented the often-considerable contributions of native converts, priests and catechists in spreading the Christian faith.[16]

---

[16] These analyses often draw on examples from West Africa, where freed slaves like the famous Bishop Crowther were particularly instrumental in promoting Christianity. However, native clergy also played active roles in other parts of the continent, such as East and Central Africa and the northern frontiers of the Cape colony (Ajayi 1965; Ayandele 1966; Beidelman 1974; Boahen 1989; Horton 1971; Opoku 1985; Ranger 1986).

The more data- and methods-driven debates that dominate recent quantitative literature on missionary work typically devote less attention to this mostly historiographical and case study–based research. However, similar concerns usually enter the discussion around questions with more tangible implications for the estimation of missionary impacts. For instance, the economic historian Ewout Frankema and other authors have warned that archival mission statistics that provide the basis for much of recent quantitative research often carry Eurocentric biases and thus, provide at best narrow, nonrepresentative snapshots of the realities of conversionary efforts on the ground (De Haas and Frankema 2018; Frankema 2012; Jedwab et al. 2022). The reason is that they were often compiled by white senior clergy who were mostly based in larger and better-connected mission centers, and thus frequently ignored or lacked information about the efforts of native converts working in more remote regions. Church archives consequently tend to overrepresent the accomplishments of expatriate missionaries, while downplaying the often-considerable African contribution in spreading Christianity. In addition, the over-sampling of better-equipped foreign-run mission centers can lead to inaccurate estimates of the impacts of missionary work. For example, Jedwab et al. (2022) compare archival sources included in Africa-wide compendiums like Roome's and Beach's mission atlases with finer-grained local church records from the former Gold Coast colony. They not only find the expected discrepancy between more centralized and local church statistics.[17] The predicted long-term economic effects of better-equipped mission stations in Roome's and Beach's maps are also almost always higher than those of smaller, less well-resourced mission outposts included in local archives.

Other recent studies document more direct negative consequences of mission presence. For instance, recent research by Okoye (2021) indicates that individuals from ethnic groups in Anglophone Africa that were more heavily exposed to missionary activity report significantly lower levels of interpersonal and intergroup trust. He links this to the disruptive influence of missionary proselytizing on local customary institutions. A companion paper to the previously cited article by Cage and Rueda engages with negative effects of the transfer of conservative norms regarding reproductive health. It suggests that, while missionary supply of medical services tends to be associated with better health care availability today, missionaries' purist views on sexuality and family structures likely delayed effective responses to new challenges like the AIDS pandemic (Cage and Rueda 2020). Yet other studies do not point to directly negative

---

[17] See Okoye (2021), Wietzke (2014, 2015), and Montgomery (2017) for similar discrepancies for Nigeria, Madagascar, and Tanzania respectively.

results but question earlier claims that mission presence had positive impacts on local economic development. For example, my own earlier research from Madagascar finds no visible effects of mission presence on a range of socioeconomic indicators, including household incomes and colonial wages (Wietzke 2015). Jedwab et al. show that positive economic impacts of missionary work that were documented in other world regions are either not observable (Jedwab et al. 2021), or not very robust to the inclusion of geographic and economic controls (Jedwab et al. 2022).

3.3 Outlook and Conclusion

The remainder of this Element returns to the interaction between missionary efforts and colonial regime contexts in sub-Saharan Africa. The purpose of this focus is not to dismiss the other critiques in the field of mission studies outlined above. However, I argue that there is still sufficient space for examining the complex interplay between the religious and colonial scrambles for Africa. Unpacking these interdependencies can foster a more critical perspective, by questioning the notion that missionaries represented a relatively neutral and apolitical "supply shock" in African societies. In many parts of the continent, the decisions and behaviors of foreign churches during the overlapping colonial and missionary struggles for hegemony had profound and long-lasting consequences for the way religious, social, and spatial relations came to be organized in African societies. Deeper analysis of these dynamics can, by itself, lead to a more nuanced assessment of mission history and its legacies in the region.

4 Theoretical Framework: Religious Markets and Religious Pluralism

This section integrates the arguments made earlier in this Element into a more coherent theoretical framework. It departs from the economics and political science literature reviewed above in two ways. First, it reextends the focus of discussion forward, to include the decades preceding the colonial partitioning of Africa. This allows incorporating determinants and consequences of religious behaviors during the early phase of the (nineteenth-century) missionary scramble, when colonial states were still largely absent. I argue that the local historical contexts and challenges encountered by church pioneers at the time are critical for understanding how missionary work unfolded during this and subsequent periods.

Second, it returns to the role of religious competition. I posit that the overlapping religious rivalries that existed during the missionary scramble shaped important aspects of missionary behavior, such as when and where new fields of proselytizing activity were opened or the strategies that were chosen to attract new converts.

The basis for my discussion is provided by previously cited sociological and economic literature that conceptualizes the behavior of faith-based organizations under the metaphor of a religious market (Berger 1963, 1969; Iannaccone 1991; Warner 1993). I argue that the emphasis that these perspectives place on competitive pressures under circumstances where religious allegiances are not yet fully settled is particularly helpful for interpreting missionary strategies during the early stages of the Christian revival in Africa. In addition, the market metaphor is useful for (re)introducing the growing importance of colonial policies into the analysis. As with any other market-like situation, the degree of competition faced by agents operating within it is determined by surrounding governing institutions. From the late nineteenth century onward, these external guardrails were mostly introduced by colonial regimes. All of the theoretical arguments developed here draw explicitly on economic concepts and terminology. They should thus be directly compatible with the quantitative economics and political science literature reviewed previously.

4.1 The Market Metaphor and its Applicability to African Mission History

The metaphor of a religious market has a long pedigree in the social sciences that extends well beyond the field of mission studies. For instance, Adam Smith already noted that the degree of "exertion, . . ., zeal and industry" of the "teachers" of religion depended critically on the presence of religious rivals (Smith 1776, cited in Iannaccone 1991, 157). Also today, the market metaphor is widely used by sociologists and economists to study contemporary variation in religious activity in regions as diverse as Europe, North, and South America. Examples include Barro and McCleary (2005), who employ it to predict cross-country differences in the emergence of state religions; Finke and Stark (1988), Iannaccone (1991), and Warner (1993), who analyze religious diversity in the United States and Europe; and Trejo (2009) and McCleary and Barro (2019) who study Protestant-Catholic relations in Latin America. However, the first and most coherent formulation of the argument is typically attributed to the sociologist Peter Berger and his now classic text *The Social Reality of Religion* (Berger 1969).

Berger developed his theory to describe conditions in post-Reformation Europe and nineteenth-and twentieth-century North America, where sociocultural processes of secularization and modernization were sufficiently advanced to undermine the religious predominance of previously hegemonic belief systems like Catholicism. He labels the resulting situation as one of "religious pluralism" and contrasts it to the preceding order of "religious monopoly" (Berger 1969, 135ff). Under the latter, only one particular faith system enjoys a dominant status in society. Moreover, these monopolies are typically "authoritatively imposed" by the "coercive support" of the state (Berger 1969, 131ff; Warner 1993, 1053). Often, it is only the marriage between a spiritually hegemonic faith and the state's coercive apparatus that keeps a dominant religion sufficiently "pure" and stable to permit it to endure over time. Historical regimes like prerevolutionary Catholic France or Calvin's Geneva are obvious examples (Berger 1969, 135). By contrast, in a "pluralistic situation," former religious monopolies are neither any longer taken for granted by large parts of the population, nor imposed by the state. This forces faith-based actors to "promote" their religion, just as economic agents would do with regular commercial goods in a normal market place. Religious organizations typically do so by providing prospective adherents with attractive "consumer goods," which can include new spiritual content or services, as well as more profane benefits, like education or health care (Berger 1969; Lankina and Getachew 2013, 108; Warner 1993). In Berger's own words, "Religious tradition . . . must be 'sold' to a clientele that is no longer constrained to 'buy'. The pluralistic situation is, above all, a market situation" (Berger 1969, 137).

As I do in this Element, a small number of studies already applied the market metaphor to the specific area of Christian missionaries. Key examples include the aforementioned work by Gallego and Woodberry (2010), who analyze interactions between colonial regimes and educational investments of Protestant and Catholics in sub-Saharan Africa. In a different regional context, Lankina and Getachew (2013) employ it to explore Protestant influences on female education supply in the southern parts of colonial India. Consistent with the above theory, both studies show that, under conditions where colonial regimes did not enforce a monopoly for any singular faith system, the provision of core services like education tends to be much higher across religions and Christian denominations.

There are, of course, legitimate questions whether the concept of a religious market that was originally developed for Western societies can or should be transferred to a context like nineteenth- and early twentieth-century Africa. Clearly, during the period of interest here, neither the development of capitalist economies nor the cultural process of secularization were sufficiently advanced in the region to apply Berger's arguments one to one. However, here and in the remainder of this Element my focus will be less on the direct applicability of the concept of a religious market as such and more on the theory's *political* and institutional content. I argue that the primary element of Berger's description of a pluralistic situation that is applicable to Africa was the lack of a state-enforced religious monopoly. As shall become clear, under these conditions, several widely observable behaviors of missionaries are actually rather well explained by Berger's theory.

The first important factor where the behavior of Christian missions was concerned, was the initial lack of a state willing or able to enforce a religious monopoly in favor of either of the two major Christian denominations. For instance, before the colonial partitioning, Western types of modern statehood only existed in rudimentary form in the continent's early European settlements. However, even here the willingness to enforce religious monopolies was uneven (Gallego and Woodberry 2010; Sundkler and Steed 2000). In other areas, Indigenous states certainly existed. Yet, they either resisted Christian influences (see e.g. the Islamic caliphates of West Africa), or they only accepted Christianity as an "official" religion so late in the precolonial period that the effects of these choices were soon disrupted by the onset of European rule.[18] In most cases, Catholics and Protestants thus faced a religious field without any monopoly to hold onto or defend. The main exceptions were the relatively small territories under former Catholic influence in Lusophone Africa. However, even here, local rulers rarely resisted the influx of Protestant pioneers from the nineteenth century onward (Sundkler and Steed 2000, 302ff).

There are strong indications that, under these conditions, missionaries really did have to "sell" the new faith (or their respective interpretation of it) to local populations. They typically did so through behaviors that are entirely compatible with the predictions of Berger's theory. For instance, the use of education by Protestants to attract local communities is relatively well acknowledged and will be discussed in more length in Section 6. Yet, also the educational investments of Catholics were impressive. Some of the most influential Catholic orders in Africa, like the White Fathers and Holy Ghost Fathers, recognized from the start that the supply of local schools was essential, both for building new generations of local priests and catechists and for winning over potential new converts (Berman 1974; Sundkler and Steed 2000).[19] They established vast

---

[18] Examples include the Ashanti and Merina empires (Ghana and Madagascar, respectively) whose rulers only converted to Christianity decades before the onset of colonialism. The relatively early conversion of the Bugandan court is an exception. However, even here Catholics and Protestants were allowed to coexist in different parts of the kingdom. Traditional belief systems likewise were too localized or weakened by the turmoils of slavery and warfare to uphold religious monopolies of their own (Rabeson 2017; Sundkler and Steed 2000).

[19] None of this is to say that Christianity did not have an intrinsic appeal to many communities. For instance, many Africans hoped that the new, seemingly powerful faith might offer a more effective remedy to the perennial problem of witchcraft than traditional religions and rituals, which had patently failed to do so (Opoku 1985; Ranger 1999). Subsections of the population, such as the young and former slaves, also embraced Christianity as a way to break through

networks of schools that became important foundations for the (frequently Catholic) faith-based education providers that persist in Africa to this day (Jennings 2013; Kitaev 1999; Wietzke 2014; Wodon 2020).[20] Moreover, contrary to common perception, much of Catholic instruction was initially offered in the local vernacular, in order to increase the attractiveness of schools to African communities (Pawliková-Vilhanová 2007; Sundkler and Steed 2000).[21] There is also ample anecdotal evidence that Catholics initiated important educational innovations, such as female and secondary schooling, when it helped attract new followers in areas where basic education was already provided by Protestants (see Gallego and Woodberry 2010 and Section 6).

The onset of colonialism in many ways made the task of conversion easier. For instance, Robin Horton notes that, once "Europeans came to be seen as symbols of power," the new faith became much more attractive to local populations. "Christianity itself came to be seen as part of a larger order, comprising Western education, colonial administration, commerce and industry, with which everyone had henceforth to reckon" (Horton 1971, 86). However, colonial rule generally did not result in the emergence of religious monopolies. While many missionaries certainly lobbied their home governments for preferential treatment, the overall success of these efforts was undermined by another indirect effect of the particular historical context of the missionary and colonial scrambles for Africa: By the time the colonial partitioning reached its climax, the process of secularization that underpins Berger's own historical account was already so far advanced in most metropolitan centers that it also affected policies in overseas territories. For instance, Britain, Germany, and the United States were so thoroughly influenced by the Reformation that they rejected the predominance of any particular Christian denomination at home or in their colonies. In France, the former duopoly of church and state had been wiped out by the anticlerical upheavals of the revolution.[22] Even in Portugal and Spain, the former stranglehold of the Catholic Church had been thoroughly

---

traditional hierarchies (Boahen 1989; Sundkler and Steed 2000). However, overall, the new religion was more attractive when it was accompanied by modern education (Berman 1974; Horton 1971).

[20] The commitment to fostering education reached as high up as the Vatican, albeit with a stronger focus on the training of local Catholic clergy. See for example, the 1919 apostolic letter *Maximum illud* by Pope Benedict XV. Also earlier, education was an important element of the work of Italian Capuchin priests in Portuguese Congo and Angola dating back to the seventeenth century (Thornton 1998).

[21] In particular the White Fathers became respected authorities in native languages (Hastings 1996; Pawliková-Vilhanová 2007). Missionaries of both denominations often only switched to European languages, once this was demanded by colonial authorities and local populations during more advanced stages of colonial rule (Berman 1974).

[22] The principle of state-church separation was further written into French law in 1905, just decades after the colonial partitioning.

weakened by the eighteenth-century expulsion of Jesuits from colonies and homeland.

The ground rules for the annexation of African lands established at the 1885 and 1890 Berlin and Brussels conferences thus resisted any trend toward religious monopoly.[23] As noted in Section 2, the closing act of Berlin contained strong language about the principles of religious liberty and impartiality. It guaranteed the right to "the free and public exercise of *all* forms of divine worship" (General Act of the Berlin Conference on West Africa, Article 6. Emphasis added). Other stipulations gave religious organizations "the right to build edifices for religious purposes, and to organize religious missions belonging to all creeds" (General Act of the Berlin Conference on West Africa, Article 6).[24]

In later years, colonial powers certainly became more intrusive, providing "favored" missions with advantages over their competitors. For instance, Portugal, Belgium, Italy, France, and Germany complicated the work of "foreign" missions, such as by requiring that instruction in religious schools should take place in the language of the colonizers. These countries also often demanded stricter quality standards and teacher diplomas, which had to be issued through the colonial administration (Section 2). Such interventions often amounted to effective advantages for Catholic missions among colonial powers with predominantly Catholic populations like France, Belgium and Portugal (Gallego and Woodberry 2010; Hastings 1996). However, it is not always easy to distinguish between religious and nationalistic forms of favoritism. For example, France often demanded the ceasing of activities by British Protestants in her newly acquired territories. Yet, local administrators typically did not require the closure of already established Protestant churches and schools altogether. Typically existing facilities simply had to be turned over to French Protestants (e.g. the Société des Missions Evangéliques de Paris, see Rabeson 2017; Zorn 2012). Germany and Belgium similarly favored missionaries from their own countries. Nonetheless, Germany in particular did so for Catholics *and* Protestants (Hastings 1996, 416; Johnson 1967; Montgomery 2017). Portugal preferred that, at least for the case of the Catholic church, all activities were to be carried out by Portuguese priests (Johnson 1967, 179ff). Yet, contrary to common perceptions, it also tolerated Protestant missions on its territories (Gallego and Woodberry 2010; Johnson 1967; Sundkler and Steed 2000). British authorities took the most hands-off approach, permitting

---

[23] Similar tendencies were visible in the charters of the League of Nations and later the United Nations (Gallego and Woodberry 2010).

[24] Article 6 of the Berlin closing act further designated missionaries as "objects of especial protection." As the coercive reach of colonial states expanded, these commitments offered a modicum of safety that was often absent during the early phases of missionary work.

significant degrees of missionary competition in their colonies (Gallego and Woodberry 2010; Johnson 1967). The primary exceptions were Muslim-dominated areas, where missionary activity was often prohibited to avoid conflicts with local religious leaders (Groves 1969). The uneven implementation of the Berlin and Brussels commitments, in short, provided opportunities for some favored missions to exploit regulations that worked in their advantage (Gallego and Woodberry 2010). However, none of this fully removed the pluralistic nature of the religious field in colonial Africa.

In the light of the above observations, I argue that adjustments to Berger's theory of the religious market need to be made in other domains. The first concerns the risk of other unintended value transfers that may arise when a concept that was initially developed for the context of Europe and North America is uncritically applied to a non-Western setting like Africa. As noted, while the theory aspires to higher levels of generalizability, Berger and other "founding fathers" of the market metaphor were clearly influenced by the experience of European history (Lankina and Getachew 2013). This applies especially to the tendency to assign particularly strong transformative functions to Protestantism. For instance, although he did not take much interest in the nuances of specific religious doctrines, Berger highlights Protestants' cultural contribution to the processes of secularization, which in itself helped bring about pluralistic situations.[25] Moreover, similar to other authors like Robert Woodberry, he acknowledges that, as a historically oppressed minority, Protestants initially fought hard for religious liberties and against the state-enforced monopoly of the Catholic church (Berger 1969; Woodberry 2012). While neither of this precludes that Protestants had monopolistic ambitions of their own,[26] both observations make Protestantism a comparatively more transformative force than Catholicism. Nonetheless, how well this reasoning applies in a context like nineteenth-century Africa is less clear. As described, Catholics and Protestants were initially *both* new arrivals to the religious field. Moreover, Catholics sometimes even had to struggle against quasi-monopolies established by Protestants in the few decades that preceded the Catholic return to Africa (Section 2).

Another problem is that the theory of competitive behaviors under conditions of religious pluralism tends to be underspecified. Guillermo Trejo (and others) note in a more recent context that proponents of a religion with monopolistic ambitions like Catholicism may react to competition through other strategies than the – comparatively costly – provision of services like education (Chesnut 2003; Trejo 2009; see also Lankina and Getachew 2013). Trejo studies the effect

---

[25] Berger mentions the "shrinkage in the scope of the sacred in reality" inherent to Protestant practice and theology as one of the core factors (Berger 1969, 111).

[26] See for example, the example of Calvinist Geneva mentioned above.

of the rise of US mainline Protestantism in contemporary Latin America and thus mentions the possibility that the previously hegemonic Catholic church could simply lobby the state to reestablish its former monopoly. While, for reasons outlined above, such a response would be less relevant in the historical context of Africa, other alternatives for reducing competition can just as easily be envisaged.

One possibility that aligns particularly well with actual historical experiences in the region is the partitioning of the continent into various mutually recognized and nonoverlapping spheres of religious influence. For instance, the Protestant principle of comity discussed in Section 2 reduced costs and competition by establishing clearly delineated geographic territories for various mission societies. This strategy is also directly compatible with Berger's own predictions about behaviors of religious organizations under conditions of pluralism. Unable to secure monopoly, a natural second-best solution is *oligopoly*. Moving into fully economic terminology, he describes this as cooperative "mergers" that are "functional in terms of rationalizing competition" (Berger 1969, 143). The resulting oligopolistic "cartels" achieve efficient responses, "by reducing the number of competing units and . . . dividing up the market between the larger units that remain" (Berger 1969, 87).[27]

There are, however, clearly embedded limits within Berger's own framework as to how far such a strategy of cooperative religious oligopoly could work. In many ways anticipating more recent critiques of alleged "neoliberal" tendencies within their theory (see e.g. Gauthier and Martikainen 2018), Berger and those who followed him, acknowledged natural boundaries in the applicability of the market metaphor in the field of religion. The economist Laurence Iannaccone puts the case particularly succinctly. He notes that the typically absolute nature of the theological and spiritual positions represented by faith-based organizations makes it impossible to stretch allegiances and religious compromises too far. As a concrete example, any single church "cannot both accept and reject the Bible as God's word, nor can it demand both an all-male priesthood and full equality of the sexes. . . . Individual churches must therefore choose positions that are at least as well defined as those of political parties" (Iannaccone 1991, 163). Collaboration and "cartelization" of the type described thus only works when there are some initial shared communalities at theological, spiritual, or even sociological level (Berger 1963, 84f, 1969). But collaboration breaks down when it puts too much strain on the underlying theological legitimizations (Berger 1969, 143).[28]

---

[27] Similar to my discussion here, Berger outlines this process in the context of modern iterations of ecumenicity and comity among American Protestant churches (Berger 1963, 1969, 140ff).

[28] To this Berger adds the self-interest of religious bureaucracies, which can further reduce incentives for mergers and collaboration (Berger 1969, 143).

I argue that these more nuanced formulations of the market metaphor describe the broad trends observable during the missionary scramble for Africa rather well. On the one hand, there clearly was a tendency toward coordination and harmonization among churches that shared core doctrinal positions. The aforementioned comity principle and tendencies towards for nondenominationalism are the prime example on the Protestant side (Hastings 1996, 246f). Similar trends existed among Catholic mission societies. While Catholic proselytizing was initially divided across multiple organizations with often strong and distinct national origins,[29] matters changed toward the end of the nineteenth century. By then, Catholic missionary efforts became increasingly centralized under the authority of the Vatican. The process culminated during the tenures of the "missionary popes" Benedict XV and Pius XI (1914–22 and 1922–39, respectively), who took a particularly active interest in the guidance and harmonization of Catholic missionary efforts. Both intervened directly in the work of individual mission societies through multiple papal encyclicals and apostolic letters and demanded a strict break with any nationalist ambitions and allegiances that persisted from earlier years.[30]

By contrast, efforts at coordination usually failed when it came to attempts of ecumenical outreach across the Protestant-Catholic divide. At local level, Catholic bishops discouraged agreements with Protestant missions around mutually recognized territorial spheres of influence (Pfisterer 1933, 162). The aforementioned "missionary popes" likewise explicitly forbade collaboration with Protestants, dismissing such attempts as "in error and deceived" and "distorting the idea of true religion."[31] Protestants on their side, had already done the same by reframing comity in explicit opposition to the Catholic church (Section 2). What dominated from the top to the bottom of internal church hierarchies was the often-intense rivalry and mutual distrust between Protestants and Catholics. These antagonisms only diminished in importance with the onset of the international ecumenical movements of the post–World War II period (Section 7).

For the remainder of my discussion, the above observations have three implications. First, where competition within the missionary movement is concerned, I distinguish here only between the broad categories of Catholicism and Protestantism. This goes against a recent tendency in economic literature to

---

[29] For example, the French White Fathers and the Italian Verona Fathers; see Section 2.

[30] See especially the apostolic letter *Maximum illud* of 1919 (www.vatican.va/content/benedict-xv/en/apost_letters/documents/hf_ben-xv_apl_19191130_maximum-illud.html), as well as Sundkler and Steed 2000, 626ff).

[31] Papal encyclical *Mortalium animos* issued 1928 by Pius XI (www.vatican.va/content/pius-xi/en/encyclicals/documents/hf_p-xi_enc_19280106_mortalium-animos.html). See also *Maximum illud* for similar content.

focus on finer-grained comparisons that also account for differences between specific "sects" or subdenominations (for instance, Franciscans, Jesuits, Baptists, and Anglicans, see e.g. Michalopoulos and Papaioannou 2020; Waldinger 2017). However, the theoretical arguments and historical evidence presented in the last paragraphs suggest that more aggregate distinction along the Catholic-Protestant divide represents a more relevant and salient perspective in the historical context of Africa.[32]

Second, I move away from the tendency of assigning a particularly transformative effects to Protestant missions. One of the core predictions of Berger's theory is that competition between rival religious organizations reduces differences in behaviors. As all missionary denominations struggled to win over new adherents, their strategies converged around activities that are likely to attract prospective converts – with education provision as the core and most widely cited example. In addition – as outlined – in the African context, pluralistic situations were not triggered by the arrival or particularly innovative behaviors of Protestants alone. With the notable exception of regions with longer-running histories of Catholic engagement (e.g. Angola and coastal parts of the Congo), Protestants and Catholics in the nineteenth century were *both* newcomers. Similarly, in areas like education, both engaged in important innovations of their own.

Finally, I follow authors like Gallego and Woodberry (2010) in treating colonialism as an increasingly important mediating factor. As seen, colonial influences became particularly visible in territories controlled by France, Portugal, and Belgium, where various regulatory interventions in favor of missions from the home country often effectively resulted in higher levels of protection for the Catholic church (Gallego and Woodberry 2010; Hastings 1996). I concur with earlier literature that, in these less competitive settings, Protestant-Catholic differences in doctrine will be more likely to result in observable consequences. However, I also posit that the failure of most colonial regimes to fully enforce religious monopolies never completely removed the pressures of religious rivalry. For instance, the fact that core principles of religious pluralism remained broadly intact even in the more interventionist colonial regimes forced Catholics to continue to make basic investments in services like education in most parts of Africa.

---

[32] My arguments also help assuage concerns about studies that distinguish only between Catholics and Protestants for pragmatic reasons. For instance, widely used sources like Nunn's digitized version of Roome's map only provide information on Protestant and Catholic missions, but do not differentiate between specific mission societies. Moreover, I argue below that finer-grained comparisons are often complicated by historical phenomena like comity that are predicted by the theory. The resulting creation of nonoverlapping territorial spheres of missionary activity naturally reduced the degree of religious competition observable in any specific location.

The remainder of this Element provides concrete examples how the above arguments matter for the recent quantitative literature on mission impacts. In the next section, I extend the use of the market metaphor forward – from the better-studied domain of "marketable goods" and services like education – to also include the prior phase where a basic physical presence of mission churches still needed to be established. I posit that inter-religious competition during these earlier stages of missionary activity is an important – yet regularly overlooked – factor in attempts to explain empirical patterns like the strong concentration of Protestant and Catholic missions in some parts of Africa (see e.g. Figure 1, Section 2). My argument matters in particular in the light of the described breakdown of interdenominational oligopolistic arrangements around mutually agreed territories of influence. In many cases, Protestants' and Catholics' decisions to open new outposts were driven *precisely* by their desire to reverse any emerging local hegemony of their respective rivals. The two major denominations, in other words, often followed each other into new territories, contributing to the clustering of mission activity.

I also show that the reluctance of colonial powers to fully enforce religious monopolies enabled these behaviors to continue after the partitioning of Africa. For instance, there are strong signs that Protestants exploited the failure of colonial powers like Portugal to protect previously hegemonic positions of the Catholic church in areas like Angola and the littoral Congo. Often, Protestant followed their rivals into these regions (Johnson 1967; Sundkler and Steed 2000, 178f, 302ff). Catholics themselves frequently sought to make up ground lost before to Protestants when a region fell under more friendly colonial regimes after the partitioning (Hastings 1996, 255, 433). In the data analyzed below, this is particularly visible in higher levels of competition between preexisting Protestant missions and Catholics in French-controlled territories.

The second example engages with the more widely researched effect of religious competition on missionary school provision. My starting point is (again) the often-made assertion that Protestants were more likely to have a transformative effect in this domain than Catholics. This claim is typically based on culturalist and norm-based arguments highlighting the formers' stronger emphasis on the literacy of lay persons (see e.g. Montgomery 2017; Nunn 2014). Without denying that such doctrinal differences existed, I predict that their consequences will be less regularly observed in the pluralistic settings that prevailed in most parts of Africa. In the presence of competition by other missionaries and faith systems, educational investments also represented an important means for Catholics to attract new converts.

My empirical research design broadly follows that of Gallego and Woodberry (2010), by exploiting variation in the extent of Catholic-Protestant competition that was permitted by different colonial regimes. However, noting that the failure to completely enforce religious monopolies never fully removed the pressure on Catholics to compete with Protestants, I focus on more specific domains of religious education provision, where doctrinal differences are more likely to yield observable consequences. The specific example I explore is female education. In this area, Catholics' ability to provide schooling at scale was influenced by other doctrinal positions that were less affected by religious competition, such as the principles of celibacy and an all-male priesthood. These norms reduced the number of female staff that often played critical roles in opening and running schools for girls (Bastian 2000; Leach 2008). The historical and econometric evidence presented below suggests that Catholic missions only overcame these added organizational disadvantages in the most competitive educational markets of Anglophone Africa. By contrast, Catholic-Protestant differences in female education remained visible in the more protectionist and interventionist regimes of French, Belgian, and German colonies (Section 6).

5 The Competitive Placement of Mission Stations

The strong concentration of missionary activity in only certain parts of the continent is one of the most striking features of the nineteenth- and early twentieth-century Christian revival in Africa. For instance, in the mission map presented in Section 2 there is a clearly visible clustering of outposts of both major denominations in the Congo, around the African Great Lakes, and in Madagascar and coastal West Africa (Figure 1). These geographic patterns are of substantive interest in their own right, as they help explain where and how Christianity and transformative influences like modern education took early roots (Nunn 2010, 2014; Wietzke 2014). However, they also pose analytical challenges for the new literature on missionary impacts. For instance, if it can be shown that missionaries systematically favored localities that were more accessible or otherwise advantaged in terms of their climatic, geographic or socioeconomic characteristics, observed associations with contemporary development outcomes will be harder to attribute to the presence of missionaries alone: any superior performance today may just reflect lingering effects of more favorable conditions in the past. Most methodological efforts in recent quantitative scholarship therefore focus on identifying and controlling for these confounding factors (see e.g. Cage and Rueda 2016; Cogneau and Moradi 2014; Dupraz 2019; Jedwab et al. 2022; Nunn 2010).

The primary issue I take in this section is with the range of variables now commonly used in this literature to predict where missionaries settled.

In particular the concern with possible locality-induced biases has often led researchers to focus mostly on structural or socioeconomic confounders that may explain both mission presence and contemporary development, such as a region's accessibility, its survivability to Europeans in the nineteenth century, or its suitability to missionaries' agricultural and economic activities. This choice of variables has had the side effect to reinforce the impression that missionary work was a relatively "apolitical supply shock" that was only driven by practical considerations and necessities. Building on the historical evidence and theoretical arguments presented in the previous sections, I argue that the competitive dimensions of missionaries' struggle for religious hegemony should be introduced as an additional factor into these analyses. While I acknowledge that other predictors commonly considered in recent literature certainly also mattered, I maintain that the competitive pressures inherent to the missionary scramble represents a hitherto underappreciated *further* influence on the geographic distribution of foreign church activity in Africa. Omitting this variable may not only cause researchers to overlook substantively important drivers of the uneven expansion of Christianity in the region. It may also lead to a misspecification of the nonrandom processes of mission placement that constitute a major source of concern in the estimation of mission impacts.

To illustrate the above points, I turn to the econometric regression frameworks that are now widely used in recent literature. In the analysis presented below, I compare the statistical effects of religious rivalry on mission placement with those of other more widely studied geographic and socioeconomic predictors. The results indicate that the statistical influence of local religious competition indeed often dominates over that of these alternative variables.

In a second step, I show that the clustering of missionary activity that was due to religious competition also interacts in somewhat unexpected ways with concerns about locality-induced biases in the estimation of missionaries long-run economic impacts. While the geographic and sociodemographic controls typically considered in the literature tend to correlate positively with contemporary economic development, I find that areas with more intense mission rivalry are often comparatively worse off today. These results underline that the consequences of the competitive processes described here should be considered as an independent factor in attempts to deal with potential biases in the evaluation of missionaries' long-term effects.

5.1 Unpacking the Determinants of Mission Placement

A good starting point for my discussion is the recent debate about determinants of mission placement that need to be accounted for in the estimation strategies adopted by the literature reviewed here. For instance, Nunn (2010) notes that mission stations were more likely to open in areas that were relatively access-ible, suitable for agricultural production and more heavily affected by the slave trade. Accordingly, his analysis of missionary impacts controls for local trans-port links, geographic conditions, and the number of slaves exported from a locality. To this, Cage and Rueda (2016) add a range of demographic vari-ables, such as historical population sizes and urbanization rates. More recently, Jedwab et al. (2022) assemble a wide set of geographic and sociodemographic determinants of mission presence that, they argue, should be accounted for in all observational analyses of the long-run effects of missionary presence. Among others, they introduce data on local climatic and disease environments, accessi-bility, precolonial population sizes and political institutions, as well as measures of agricultural suitability. Consistent with the authors' expectation, the inclu-sion of these controls significantly reduces (but does not remove) the estimated effect of mission presence on long-term economic development.

From the point of view of my argument, the primary shortcoming of the above analyses is their failure to consider the impacts of religious rivalry on mission placement. For example, in the studies by Nunn (2010) and Jedwab et al. (2022), missionaries of all major denominations are simply added up into one summary measure.[33] Where the competition between Catholics and Protestants is concerned, this approach captures effects of religious rivalry at best indirectly. However, it cannot be ruled out that high numbers of mission outposts on the resulting variable may just reflect the concentration of resources by one single denomination. By contrast, it becomes impossible to determine whether decisions of a particular church to open new outposts were influenced by the presence of a rival mission or not. As a further problem, all of the (Africa-wide) analyses cited above fail to distinguish between different colonial regime contexts. This makes it harder to account for the effect of diverging colonial policies on the extent of local religious competition after the partitioning (Sections 2 and 4).

The available historical evidence suggests that the nonconsideration of reli-gious rivalries can lead to very incomplete accounts of why missionary activity was so unevenly distributed in Africa. For example, Johnson (1967, 171) notes that the concentration of Protestant and Catholic outposts in Central Africa near present-day Uganda, Rwanda and Burundi is not adequately explained by often-emphasized structural conditions like geographic accessibility. On the contrary, in their race to Africa's interior, competing missions arrived in the region from

---

[33] My own earlier work on missionaries in Madagascar is also culpable of this, see Wietzke (2014, 2015).

different directions and via different access routes. In places like the coastal Congo and Angola, initial Protestant activity was explained by the desire to break the quasi-monopoly of the Catholic church that existed as a legacy of earlier Portuguese colonization (Sundkler and Steed 2000). Inversely, in Madagascar, Catholics followed Protestants in a quest to offset the former's advantage in the island. Much of this rivalry played out in the country's rugged and relatively inaccessible interior, where missions of both denominations competed for influence over the locally dominant Merina kingdom (Rabeson 2017; Wietzke 2015).

Also where the question of location-induced statistical biases is concerned, the implications of the described competitive behaviors are not always straightforward. On the one hand, religious rivalry certainly did reinforce the concentration of mission activity in areas that had particularly favorable attributes. This happened, for instance, when late-coming churches chose to settle in locations that were considered as attractive by mission pioneers in the past. However, the same multiplier effects can easily bolster the clustering of missionary work in more disadvantaged regions. It is widely recognized that many missions deliberately targeted populations that were particularly destitute or set back by other influences, like the slave trade (Johnson 1967; Nunn 2010; Waldinger 2017). Also in subsequent periods, mission societies and churches across the continent often worked under explicit humanitarian and poverty-focused objectives (Groves 1969; Jennings 2013). Finally, discrepancies with local economic development potentials frequently emerged from the often-limited spatial overlap between missionary and colonial activity. In particular more conservative missionaries of both major denominations often preferred to work further away from larger European settlements, as outlined in Section 2. In addition, in their rush for new souls and converts, missionaries tended to compete most intensively in areas that were more densely populated in the precolonial period (Jedwab et al. 2022; Johnson 1967). These type of regions were typically avoided by other Europeans and thus did not benefit from the "reversal of fortunes" often associated with settler-intense forms of colonialism (Acemoglu et al. 2002; Wietzke 2015). My analysis below suggests that these various mismatches between local mission presence and a region's long-term economic potential can indeed change the direction of bias in estimates of missionaries' long-run development impacts.

5.2 Empirical Analysis

The following analysis illustrates that the consequences of missionary rivalry are also traceable in the quantitative research designs that are now widely employed in the new interdisciplinary literature on missionary impacts. My empirical approach aligns with the Africa-wide studies of Nunn (2010) and Jedwab et al. (2022), in that it draws on Roome's mission atlas as the primary source of information on historical mission presence (see Figure 1). As noted previously, Roome's map provides one of the most widely used sources for quantitative analyses of historical missionary work in the region. While Roome's data tend to underreport the presence of smaller outposts that were run by native converts (see Section 3.2), I regard this focus on European mission stations as less problematic for my present purposes. Based on the map, it should still be possible to capture the strategic location choices of *white* churchmen and –women, who were generally the main perpetrators of the missionary scramble for Africa.

Following Jedwab et al. (2022), I divide the map into geographically and politically "neutral" grid cells for the purposes of estimation.[34] However, the cells used here are larger (0.5 degrees in latitude and longitude, instead of the 0.1 × 0.1 degrees used by Jedwab et al.). The cell sizes in my analysis approximate 50 × 50 km at the equator. This is large enough to pick up effects of competitive mission placement in areas where churches' location choices were regulated by colonial powers. For example, Gallego and Woodberry (2010, 304) note that Portuguese authorities in present-day Angola and Mozambique restricted the operation of Protestant missions within a radius of approximately 20 miles of the next to Catholic station. British authorities similarly imposed a five-mile radius between missions of different denominations in South Africa to avoid conflicts (Sundkler and Steed 2000, 403). Cells approximating 50 km in width and length should still capture competing missions of the respective other denomination in these contexts.[35]

The two dependent variables are, respectively, the cell count of Protestant and Catholic mission stations in 1924. My primary predictor for the influence of religious competition is the number of mission stations of the respective other denomination (Catholic or Protestant) in the same cell. In an attempt to capture which missions reached a location first, I use data for earlier time periods for these latter two variables. For Protestant missions this draws on Beach's atlas, who reports the location of mission stations in 1903. For Catholics it is based on historical data for 1889 by Leon Bethune. Both variables were georeferenced and made publically available by Cage and Rueda (2016).

---

[34] The underlying grid structure and many of the geographic controls used below are from Tollefsen et al. (2012).

[35] Note that not *all* competing mission around these perimeters will be included in the same cell. Consequently, my analysis represents conservative approximations of the true extent of intermissionary rivalry.

For practical reasons, this part of my analysis largely ignores the competition with Islam. One primary challenge is that historical cartography typically only describes Muslim areas as a large geographic sphere.[36] By contrast, these sources do not provide disaggregated information about local Muslim population shares or religious sites (e.g. mosques) that would be required for the finer-grained subnational analysis implemented here. In addition, in regions like West Africa, colonial regulations often declared large swathes of majority-Muslim territories off-limits to missionaries. This reduced the extent of localized competition of the type targeted by the grid-cell structure described above. Nonetheless, adopting a strategy first employed by Nunn (2010), I show in the Element's Annex that my results also hold when I exclude regions of Africa with historically larger Muslim populations (Table A2).

As indicated, my analysis compares the effects of missionary competition against a range of geographic and socioeconomic controls that are now widely used as predictors of mission presence in the literature. For ease of presentation, I divide these into three categories:

1. *Accessibility.* Before the onset of systematic investments in modern transport infrastructure, missionaries faced severe obstacles in reaching more remote areas. I account for these challenges through a range of measures of a location's accessibility in the early colonial period. These include a cell's distance to the cost, the presence of colonial railways in 1911, and the proximity of explorer routes (see Figure 1). My analysis expands on previous literature by also controlling for the availability of mission stations of the same denomination in a region. This addresses the fact that many missionary societies responded to the logistical challenges of nineteenth-century Africa by working out of interconnected chains of mission stations. Under this strategy, larger and more connected mission centers served as relays to transfer personnel and supplies from the coast to more remote outposts (Johnson 1967; Nunn 2010). The variable also provides an alternative measure of mission concentration that is less likely to be driven by religious competition. The control used in this context is the count of mission stations of the same denomination within a grid cell and its eight neighboring cells.

2. *Health and Geographic Conditions.* Missionaries in the nineteenth and early twentieth century in Africa suffered extremely high rates of illness and mortality, as they did not yet benefit from subsequent innovations in tropical medicine (e.g. the introduction of penicillin or chloroquine, Nunn 2010).

---

[36] These usually broadly cover North Africa down to the Sahel and the continent's east coast down to Tanzania (see e.g. Ajayi and Crowder 1985).

Much of early missionary activity was thus restricted to healthier and more temperate regions. Missionaries further depended on fertile and relatively well-irrigated land to cultivate crops for their sustenance and commerce (Jedwab et al. 2022; Johnson 1967; Nunn 2010). In my analysis, these factors are approximated by a grid cell's average historical Malaria burden,[37] terrain characteristics (share of mountainous and barren land), and climatic conditions (temperature, frequency of droughts, length of rainy season).

3. *Sociodemographic Characteristics.* Historians highlight that missionaries preferred to build churches and schools in the most populous areas and among communities that lived more sedentary lifestyles. Larger populations offered more people to convert, while nonnomadic societies made it easier to establish permanent mission stations (Groves 1969; Johnson 1967). This is reflected in well-documented positive associations between mission presence and historical population densities (Cage and Rueda 2016; Jedwab et al. 2022; Nunn 2010). I account for this through local population estimates for 1900 from the HYDE project (Klein Goldewijk et al. 2011), a control for ethnic groups that had a city with a population above 20, 000 inhabitants in 1850, and a binary indicator for nomadic and seminomadic populations. The presence of societies that had centralized forms of political organization is also included, given well-known associations between historical statehood and the demographic and economic development of a region (Herbst 2000).[38] Finally, I draw on Nunn (2008) for data on the local population's exposure to the slave trade. This addresses the fact that missionaries tended to target their educational and economic activities to regions that were more heavily affected by slave raids (see above).

The econometric analysis is based on a negative binomial regression model to account for the large number of zero values in the dependent variable. Standard errors are clustered at the level of colonial territories to address possible influences of colonial institutions (I use borders before World War I). Extended versions of the estimation model also include controls and interactions with colonial regime types to further account for the effects of colonial regulations on mission activity (see below). All continuous independent

---

[37] I use an indicator from Depetris-Chauvin and Weil (2018). Another disease variable, the local suitability for the Tsetse Fly consistently yielded insignificant estimates and was removed from the analysis.

[38] This is measured by the number of levels of jurisdictional hierarchies above the community. This and other socio-demographic variables (except population estimates from HYDE) are from Murdock's (1967) Ethnographic Atlas and are measured as the value for the dominant ethnic group in a grid cell.

variables have been standardized to facilitate comparisons between predictors. However, qualitatively similar results were obtained when all variables were transformed into their natural logs.

5.2.1 Results

I begin by discussing results for the above geographic and sociodemographic controls (Table 1, Columns 1 and 2). First, the presence of missions of the same denomination has a consistently strong and significant effect. This finding supports the notion that proselytizing efforts typically expanded out of already operational centers of missionary activity. Other measures of a locality's accessibility, such as its distance to the coast or the presence of explorer routes and railways also have a visible influence on mission presence. However, these coefficients usually only meet the commonly accepted significance thresholds in the case of Protestant missions. This possibly reflects the latter's pioneering role during the nineteenth-century Christian revival in Africa.

Moving beyond the above measures of accessibility, there is also support for the often-noted observation that missionaries of both denominations preferred historically more populated and developed areas. The effect of local population densities is always positive and significant. In addition, missionary activity was more common among nonnomadic populations and groups that had more advanced precolonial states. However, these effects are again stronger and more consistently significant for Protestants.

The results for the geographic and climatic controls are more ambivalent. The primary exception is the share of barren land, which emerges as a strong and significant negative influence on mission presence. Note however, that the lack of statistical significance on the other variables within this segment may have to do with problems of collinearity, due to the large number of parameters included in the model. For example, disease environments, climatic conditions and terrain attributes like mountains and barrenness are typically highly intercorrelated.

Notwithstanding the large set of controls included in the model, the presence of missions of competing denominations always emerges as a strong and significant additional predictor. In the case of Protestant missions, the effect of the presence of Catholics is actually larger than that of the proximity of other Protestant missions in neighboring cells. Recall that the latter variable captures a pragmatic response to the logistical challenges of proselytizing activity in early colonial-era Africa. As such, this result underlines the importance of religious competition, relative to the more practical determinants of mission placement typically emphasized in recent literature. For Catholics the influence

Table 1 Determinants of mission placement

Dependent variable	(1) Protestant missions	(2) Catholic missions	(3) Protestant missions	(4) Catholic missions
Distance to coast	−0.300**	−0.263	−0.377***	−0.306*
	(0.141)	(0.207)	(0.118)	(0.169)
Explorer route	0.285**	0.263	0.214*	0.271*
	(0.133)	(0.162)	(0.114)	(0.151)
Railway line	0.476***	0.106	0.321**	0.076
	(0.135)	(0.319)	(0.153)	(0.347)
Population nineteenth century	0.048***	0.034**	0.050***	0.038**
	(0.006)	(0.015)	(0.008)	(0.017)
Precolonial centralization	0.174**	0.186**	0.191***	0.172
	(0.076)	(0.092)	(0.074)	(0.105)
Nomadic/seminomadic	−0.217***	0.037	−0.295***	0.014
	(0.068)	(0.090)	(0.068)	(0.080)
City in 1850	0.081*	−0.001	0.077*	0.023
	(0.045)	(0.098)	(0.045)	(0.106)
Malaria Burden	0.096	0.199*	−0.026	0.089
	(0.107)	(0.109)	(0.102)	(0.141)
Slave exports pre-1800	0.001	0.022	0.014	0.028
	(0.031)	(0.027)	(0.043)	(0.032)

	(1)	(2)	(3)	(4)
Mountains	0.095	0.170*	0.096	0.138
	(0.096)	(0.096)	(0.094)	(0.094)
Barren land	−1.037***	−1.975***	−0.993***	−1.827***
	(0.372)	(0.379)	(0.299)	(0.350)
Temperature	−0.114	0.440**	−0.046	0.599***
	(0.120)	(0.207)	(0.112)	(0.220)
Droughts	−0.002	0.155	0.047	0.135
	(0.047)	(0.102)	(0.032)	(0.095)
Length of rainy season	−0.059	0.004	−0.043	0.020
	(0.083)	(0.095)	(0.074)	(0.107)
Missions of same confession in neighboring cells	**0.211***	**0.225***	**0.198***	**0.212***
	(0.026)	**(0.036)**	**(0.025)**	**(0.038)**
Competing missions in same cell	**0.239***	**0.092***	**0.251***	**0.089***
	(0.040)	**(0.006)**	**(0.040)**	**(0.006)**
French colonyXcompeting mission			−0.059	**0.348**
			(0.068)	**(0.147)**
Spanish/Portuguese/Italian colonyX competing mission			**0.182**	0.071
			(0.092)	(0.048)
German/Belgian colonyXcompeting mission			**0.421***	0.026
			(0.054)	(0.027)

Table 1 (cont.)

Dependent variable	(1) Protestant missions	(2) Catholic missions	(3) Protestant missions	(4) Catholic missions
French colony			−0.816***	−0.481
			(0.252)	(0.356)
Spanish, Portuguese, Italian colony			−0.782**	−0.101
			(0.368)	(0.437)
German or Belgian colony			−0.011	0.508
			(0.211)	(0.389)

Coefficient estimates from a negative binomial regression model. $N = 6{,}718$ grid cells. See main text for detailed variable descriptions. Constant term not reported. Standard errors account for clustering at the level of colonial states in 1914 and are reported in parentheses. *** $p < 0.01$, ** $p < 0.05$, * $p < 0.1$. Statistically significant coefficients for key explanatory variables are in bold typeface.

of rival missions is smaller but still highly significant. Overall, these results provide strong support for the claim that competition with the respective other major denomination contributed to the decision to open a mission station in a locality.

Estimates in Columns 3 and 4 also account for colonial influences. They do so by augmenting the regression model with a control for the identity of the dominant colonial power in a grid cell before World War I, and an interaction term between this variable and the measure of missions of the respective competing denomination. (In Table 1, these are named "identity of colonial powerXcompeting mission", e.g. "French colonyXcompeting mission" for French-controlled territories).[39] German and Belgian colonies are grouped into one category, because they adopted a relatively similar approach to the freedom of movement of missions (see Section 4 and Johnson 1967). Portuguese, Italian and Spanish territories are also combined into one group, since they had comparatively longer histories of Catholic involvement and tended to favor Catholic missions (Gallego and Woodberry 2010). French and British-controlled territories are included as two individual categories, given their numeric importance in the sample. British-controlled territories serve as the reference category as they adopted the least-interventionist approach toward missionaries (Section 4).

The results of the noninteracted colonial controls in Column 3 support the often-made observation that Protestant missions were less common in territories held by powers that favored Catholics, like Italy, Portugal and Spain (see e.g. Frankema 2012; Gallego and Woodberry 2010). However, the positive and significant effect of the interaction term implies that, if Protestants decided to go to these areas, they were much more likely to target localities that already had a Catholic mission presence. These results support the claim that also Protestants were unwilling to cede ground lost previously to Catholics in regions like the coastal Congo or Angola. German- and Belgian-controlled territories emerge as a slightly more ambiguous category. The insignificant results on the noninteracted control for these colonies suggest that there were no average differences in the likelihood of Protestant and Catholic presence. However, the large and highly significant coefficient on the interaction term in Column 3 suggests that also here Protestants competed fiercely in Catholic mission areas. Again, this is consistent with historical evidence. As discussed previously, both of these colonial powers intervened heavily in the religious field and Belgium in particular tended to favor Catholic priests. Yet, both

---

[39] Each cell is assigned to the colonial power that controlled the majority of its land surface.

countries also tolerated missions of both denominations in their overseas territories, enabling this type of localized competition (Johnson 1967).

In the case of Catholic missionaries, the results point to similar influences of colonial regimes after the partitioning. Judging from the newly added colonial controls and interaction terms, Catholic competition with Protestant missions was particularly strong in French-Africa (Column 4). It is important to highlight that many of these regions already had a meaningful Protestant presence by the time they were permanently attributed to France after the Berlin and Brussels conferences. Relevant examples include Madagascar, Guinea and the French-Congo, which all had sizeable numbers of Protestant missions by the end of the nineteenth century. In these areas, the catchup played by Catholics most likely reflects overlaps between missionaries' religious and nationalist instincts discussed in Section 2. For instance, Hastings points out that the White Fathers – one of the most influential French missionary organizations – "were happy enough to see their work as one which facilitated the French conquest" (Hastings 1996, 430). The French government on its side reciprocated, as it preferred to have French missionaries in its territories (Hastings 1996 and Section 4).

The above results support my argument that the missionary and colonial scrambles for Africa represented two interrelated processes. In addition, they further back the claim that the clustering of missionary activity documented here is not driven by geographic factors alone. While it is entirely possible that Catholics and Protestants at times ended up in the same place because of a location's desirable attributes, it is highly unlikely that these factors would have weighted so unevenly across different colonial regime contexts. Political environments and missionaries' strategic behaviors within them clearly mattered as well.

5.3 Predicted Effects on Contemporary Development Outcomes

The remainder of the section explores how the clustering of mission stations that is due to religious competition may influence the estimation of the long-run developmental impacts of missionary work. The outcome of interest is now the intensity of nightly light emissions from a grid cell. This variable is a widely employed proxy measure for local economic development (Donaldson and Storeygard 2016). It is also used by Jedwab et al. (2022) in their tests of previously omitted geographic controls on estimates of the long-term socioeconomic impacts of missionary work.

Below, I estimate two models. The first includes the number of Catholic and Protestant missions in a cell, as well as the interaction term between these two variables. I treat this interaction as the primary measure of the extent of local inter-missionary competition in a locality. The second model also includes the interaction term. However, in it the controls for Protestant and Catholic missions are added up into a single summary measure. I report this model to sharpen the contrast to earlier studies like Nunn (2010) and Jedwab et al. (2022) that used a similar summary variable of mission presence (see above). It is worth dwelling briefly on the different properties of these two variables. The summary measure in the second model simply provides the sum total of missions of either denomination in a grid cell. By contrast, the interaction term is the mathematical product of the cell count of Protestant and Catholic missions. As such this variable zooms in on localities where there was Catholic-Protestant competition. In cells where either Protestants or Catholics were absent, values are sent to zero. Nonzero values are observed only in areas where missions of both denominations existed.

Further below, in Table 3, I also report extended versions of the two regression models augmented by the same set of geographic and sociodemographic variables as in Column 1 of Table 1. Finally, following Jedwab et al. (2022) all of my estimates include fixed effects and clustered standard errors at country level.[40] Differences between alternative colonial contexts were not discernable or less robust in this part of the analysis. Consequently, they are not reported. All variables have again been standardized. However, similar results were obtained with log-transformed values.

Before I turn to the results, it is helpful to briefly restate the directionality of the potential biases that could emerge from the competition-induced clustering of missions stations. As noted before, my expectations on this question are actually undefined. On the one hand, religious competition may reinforce the clustering of proselytizing activity in relatively more advantaged locations, if late-coming missions followed earlier church pioneers into areas with more favorable conditions. This would imply a positive coefficient on the interaction between Protestants and Catholics. On the other hand, inter-missionary rivalry may also lead to a concentration of missionary work in more impoverished regions, if there were deliberate efforts by pioneering missions to target relatively more disadvantaged populations. The result would be a negative coefficient on the interaction between Protestants and Catholics.

A look at the descriptive data for this analysis suggests that, in the Africa-wide sample considered here, the direction of the effects of competition leans toward more disadvantaged areas. Table 2 presents the correlation matrix between the individual cell counts of Protestant and Catholic missions, the

---

[40] Similar results were obtained without the fixed effects.

Table 2 Correlation matrix

	Nighlight emissions	Protestant missions in cell	Catholic missions in cell	Summary measure (Protestant + Catholic missions)	Interaction term (Protestant × Catholic missions)
Nighlight emissions	1.000				
Protestant missions in cell	0.249	1.000			
Catholic missions in cell	0.038	0.274	1.000		
Summary measure	0.211	0.901	0.664	1.000	
CatholicsXProtestant missions	0.023	0.358	0.572	0.537	1.000
Protestant missions in neighboring cells	0.218	0.428	0.119	0.386	0.071
Catholic missions in neighboring cells	−0.018	0.136	0.248	0.218	0.034
Distance to coast	−0.217	−0.135	−0.047	−0.126	−0.041
Explorer route	−0.004	0.016	0.027	0.025	−0.003
Railway line	0.279	0.125	0.016	0.104	−0.002

City in 1850	0.356	0.149	0.033	0.130	-0.002
Precolonial centralization	0.171	0.057	0.022	0.054	0.016
Nomadic/ seminomadic	-0.112	-0.121	-0.071	-0.126	-0.027
Population nineteenth century	0.352	0.341	0.073	0.298	0.085
Malaria Burden	-0.082	0.080	0.107	0.111	0.045
Slave exports pre-1800	-0.008	0.065	0.096	0.094	0.054
Mountains	0.001	0.041	0.017	0.040	-0.004
Barren land	-0.012	-0.132	-0.095	-0.146	-0.024
Temperature	-0.149	-0.056	0.016	-0.037	0.019
Droughts	-0.093	-0.049	-0.012	-0.043	-0.038
Length of rainy season	0.047	0.000	-0.010	-0.005	-0.013
Urban share today	0.571	0.190	0.059	0.174	0.025
Population density today	0.647	0.393	0.170	0.382	0.140
Distance to capital	-0.153	-0.122	-0.073	-0.127	-0.038

summary measure and interaction of Catholics and Protestants, and the geographic and demographic controls that were included in the previous analysis.

The noninteracted terms for Protestant and Catholic missions and the summary measure tend to correlate positively with most potential indicators of local economic development. This applies in particular to accessibility-related controls, such as colonial railway lines, explorer routes, and some of the historical sociodemographic variables like the presence of precolonial cities. These results are consistent with the regression estimates in Table 1. They also support more broadly the often-made claim that missions tended to cluster in more developed areas (Jedwab et al. 2022; Nunn 2010).

Interestingly, the pattern looks very different for the interaction between Protestant and Catholic missions. In the case of the variables above, the correlations are smaller or even negative. Also associations with other common indicators of a location's relative advantage, such as distance to the coast or to contemporary capitals (a control used in additional robustness tests below) are much weaker than for the noninteracted terms. This suggests that it was not unusual for missionaries to also compete in areas that were relatively inaccessible or in other ways less well-integrated into the emerging modern market economies of colonial states. While I refrain from claiming that these trends are directly generalizable to other historical and geographic contexts, the results are consistent with evidence above that the spatial and social organization of the missionary scramble did not always align perfectly with colonial economic activities.

The regression results also bear out these observations. The noninteracted terms for Catholic and Protestant missions have the expected positive effect on contemporary development. By contrast, the sign of the interaction term between Catholic and Protestant missions is significant and negative (Table 3, Column 1). The second model with the summary measure for Catholics and Protestants only reinforces this contrast (Column 2). Little surprisingly, the summary measure itself has the same positive coefficient as its two subcomponents in the previous model. While the significance level of the interaction term is reduced to just above 5 percent, the effect size has increased and remains negative. The inclusion of other geographic and historical controls in Columns 3 and 4 reduces the strength of the interaction term but it also tends to increase its significance. Of the noninteracted measures, the presence of Catholic missions no longer passes the commonly accepted statistical thresholds.

It should be clear from my discussion so far that I do not attribute the above findings to a direct causal (negative) effect of inter-missionary competition on economic development. Instead, in the data used here, the results underscore the negative or weaker association that often existed between heightened instances

Table 3 Effects on economic development

	(1)	(2)	(3)	(4)
Protestant missions in cell	0.186**		0.062***	
	(0.076)		(0.018)	
Catholic missions in cell	0.276**		0.202	
	(0.128)		(0.134)	
Summary measure (Catholics		0.856**		0.307***
+ Protestants)		(0.325)		(0.074)
Interaction (Catholics ×	−0.079**	−0.110*	−0.041**	−0.046**
Protestants)	(0.039)	(0.056)	(0.019)	(0.022)
Controls	No	No	Yes	Yes
R-squared	0.202	0.197	0.351	0.351

Dependent variable: nightlight emissions. Columns 3 and 4 include the same controls as Column 1 in Table 1. See Annex for full results and robustness tests. Linear regression with country fixed effects and clustered standard errors at country level (in parentheses). $N = 6,718$ *** $p < 0.01$, ** $p < 0.05$, * $p < 0.1$.

of local mission rivalry and other locality-specific correlates of long-run development. Nonetheless, the analysis presented here does underline that it is worthwhile to consider the effects of religious competition as an independent source of potential bias in the estimation of missionary impacts.

The Online Annex for this Element presents further robustness tests. Because of often-voiced concerns that the dependent variable of nightlight emissions may confound local urbanization rates and "genuine" economic development (Donaldson and Storeygard 2016), I estimate a model that includes contemporary urbanization rates and population densities. The inclusion of these controls increases the statistical significance of the interaction between Catholics and Protestants, while the noninteracted measures of Protestants alone is no longer distinguishable from zero. The Annex also demonstrates that the results for missionary competition are robust when I use local GDP estimates instead of nightlight emissions as an alternative dependent variable (Nordhaus 2006) and when I test for possible missspecifications in the model's functional form due to diminishing economic effects of larger numbers of mission stations.

5.4 Conclusion

This section explored the determinants of the uneven expansion of missionary work in nineteenth- and early twentieth-century Africa. I have moved beyond more widely studied "structural" and socioeconomic predictors of mission presence and highlighted instead the role of interdenominational competition as a further determinant for where new fields of proselyting activity were opened. Estimates in the last section illustrate that resulting imbalances in the distribution of mission stations can lead to unexpected biases in the estimation of long-run effects of local conversionary and educational efforts. In the data considered here, the drivers of inter-missionary rivalry did not correlate with other locality-specific confounders that received more attention in the recent literature on mission impacts.

As noted, my findings also have wider substantive implications. Rather than treating missionary work as a relatively "neutral" supply shock that was only shaped by practical and economic considerations, Christian expansion emerges here as a process that had inherently more strategic and even political dimensions. These are closely related to the overlapping nature of the missionary and colonial scrambles that are a core theme of this Element. In particular, I find strong evidence that regulation of religious freedoms enacted by different colonial powers had a direct effect on the intensity of local missionary competition. The next section will continue with the analysis of these colonial influences, focusing on the equally important domain of religious education.

6 Determinants of Missionary Female Education Supply

As noted in Section 3, one reason why missionary work received growing attention outside of the fields of theology and church history is the fact that it represents a process that was in many ways distinct from that of colonial state building. Whereas colonial powers shaped local outcomes from the top down, by imposing new legal and economic regimes, missionaries typically changed societal relations from the bottom up, by altering social, religious, and cultural norms. Leading protagonists of the new interdisciplinary literature reviewed here, such Nathan Nunn, argue that this makes missionary work a topic of particular interest. By studying the legacies of missionary interventions we can learn about impacts of culture and social institutions that are now a growing concern to researchers in economics and other social science disciplines (Guiso et al. 2006; Helmke and Levitsky 2004; Nunn 2010).

An area where the interest in the cultural and norm-based dimensions of missionary activity has become particularly visible is the field of female education. Researchers like Nunn often point to Protestants' insistence that men *and* women should be able to read the Bible. Resulting higher investments by Protestant missions in girls' schooling have been linked to reduced gender gaps in education (Montgomery 2017; Nunn 2014), improved long-term mobility prospects for women (Meier zu Selhausen 2014; Meier zu Selhausen and

Weisdorf 2016), and, more broadly, higher school attainments in former Protestant mission areas (Alesina et al. 2021; Cage and Rueda 2016). Catholic doctrine, by contrast, placed less emphasis on the literacy of lay persons and it promoted more conservative gender norms within the church. Accordingly, Catholic mission presence is typically identified as a cause of larger educational gender gaps (Montgomery 2017; Nunn 2014).

In keeping with the market-based theory of this Element, I posit that this juxtaposition between Protestant and Catholic approaches to female education is often too strong. On the one hand, there is ample historiographic evidence that Protestants too held very conservative gender norms (Bastian 2000; Leach 2008). In addition, differences relative to Catholics typically diminished further whenever there was strong competition between rival missions. In these latter cases, Catholics were just as willing to provide schooling to girls (and to the population more broadly), if it helped winning over new converts. The pressure to do so was particularly visible in areas where colonial powers did little to protect the position of Catholics, such as in British-controlled Africa (Gallego and Woodberry 2010; Lankina and Getachew 2013).

In this section, I test the above claim of competition-based theory by complementing earlier research by Nathan Nunn on mission-induced gender inequalities with a comparativist perspective that is explicit about differences in the degree of Protestant-Catholic competition permitted by various colonial regimes. Expanding on the aforementioned earlier research by Gallego and Woodberry (2010), I focus in particular on the diverging policies of former British colonies –as an example of a relatively unregulated market for religious education – and French, Portuguese, and German territories – as settings where Catholics enjoyed relatively stronger protection. My econometric results suggest that higher levels of competition indeed diminished the effects of differences in doctrine. On average, male-to-female educational attainments converge more strongly across Catholic and Protestant mission areas in the formerly more competitive markets of British colonies than in the more interventionist regimes of France, Portugal, and Germany. These findings again point to more context-dependent variation in missionary behaviors and their long-run impacts than would emerge from frameworks that pay less attention to the historical and institutional circumstances of missionary activity.

6.1 Existing Evidence

Diverging Protestant and Catholic approaches to education more generally – and female schooling in particular – have long been a matter of great interest to economists. A widely cited paper by Becker and Woessmann (2009) points to

Luther's emphasis on literacy as a means for personal betterment and engagement with the Gospel to explain the faster shift to mass education in historically Protestant areas. In the authors' own analysis from Reformation-era Europe, the resulting higher rates in skills and human capital accumulation alone are sufficient for explaining faster growth in Protestant regions over following periods. The argument is of wider theoretical interest because it shifts the focus from Max Weber's more opaque notion of a Protestant work ethic to tangible factors like education and human capital as the primary determinant of diverging long-run developments in Protestant and non-Protestant areas. Becker and Woessman also extend this argument explicitly to the question of female education. They note that Luther's own writing implored that girls ought to be "taught the Gospel for an hour each day," to enable them to engage with the Christian faith (Becker and Woessmann 2008, 780 citing Martin Luther). In their own analysis, the effects of this position become visible in increased supply of girls' schools and higher levels of female educational attainment, even centuries later (Becker and Woessmann 2008).

Researchers like Nathan Nunn have extended Becker's and Woessmann's arguments to the work of Protestant missionaries in Africa. Nunn follows the former two authors in highlighting Protestants' more favorable approach to female education (Nunn 2014). To explore how these norms mattered, he traces effects of historical mission presence on contemporary gender-differentiated educational outcomes in eighteen African countries. Consistent with his expectations, he finds that women's school attainments today are on average higher in areas and among groups that were more strongly exposed to Protestant missionaries. Montgomery (2017) provides similar results, based on finer-grained analysis from German East Africa (present-day Tanzania). In a slightly different research design, Meier zu Selhausen and Weisdorf (2016) draw on data from Protestant marriage registries in historical Kampala. They show that – after some lag – women also benefited from missionary schooling and often even managed to enter into white-collar and paid work (Meier zu Selhausen 2014).[41]

By contrast, Catholic missionaries' approach to female education is typically described as more restrictive. Most authors point out that Catholic doctrine only assigns marginal roles to women in church and society. In addition, they highlight that scripture reading is to be carried out by skilled priests and catechists, but not by laypersons, let alone women. The typical conclusion is that Catholic missionaries put less emphasis on whether women were able to read the Bible or not (Gallego and Woodberry 2010; Nunn 2014; Woodberry 2004). Turning to specific strategies of conversion, others note that Catholic priests generally found it

---

[41] Much of this was through church-based employment.

more acceptable to pressure people into the new faith, rather than to try and win them over through the provision of education to girls and other disadvantaged groups (Mkenda 2018; Montgomery 2017; Pfisterer 1933).

The above observations offer useful insights into missionaries' diverging normative approaches to female education. However, in their sharp distinction between Protestant and Catholic doctrine, they also tend to gloss over more complex realities on the ground. Before turning to the influence of religious competition, I briefly discuss other emerging evidence that suggests that differences between Catholics and Protestants were not always as clear cut as the above literature suggests.

Where missionaries' general approach to education is concerned, sweeping generalizations that Catholics tended to be less concerned about the literacy of laypersons are increasingly hard to maintain. This happens even within the economic literature reviewed here. For instance, several carefully executed studies show that, just like Protestants, Catholic orders like Franciscans, Dominicans, Augustinians, and Jesuits made important efforts to educate local populations (Caicedo 2018; Waldinger 2017; Wantchekon et al. 2015). Historical evidence discussed in Sections 2 and 4 similarly indicates that leading Catholic missions in Africa like the White Fathers and the Congregation of the Holy Spirit maintained vast school networks. These interventions included education for girls, which was often supplied through specialized female-led Catholic organization, such as the White Sisters (Smythe 2007; Sundkler and Steed 2000, 104f).

Also in terms of the content and quality of female education provided, differences between Protestants and Catholics were usually not that strong. As outlined in Section 2.2, missionaries of both denominations often hailed from modest educational backgrounds and frequently struggled to free themselves from the conservative role models and gender norms of their time. White Protestants and Catholics *both* thought that the appropriate place for women was the home. For instance, Leach (2008, 335) notes that Anglican missionaries in West Africa were major purveyors of the ideal of "white middle class womanhood . . ., with its emphasis on domesticity, conjugal fidelity and self-lessness" (see also Bastian 2000; Hastings 1996). Comparable descriptions exist for Catholics, such as in the case of Belgian "foyer sociaux," which trained young women in household chores to prepare them for marriage or future work as domestic aids (see e.g. Hunt 1990), as well as for Catholic schools in Senegal (Barthel 1985), and for Catholics and Protestant facilities in German East Africa (Beidelman 1974; Montgomery 2017).

In the light of this more nuanced evidence, one often has to turn to other factors to explain differences in female education provision by Catholics and Protestants. For instance, some crucial elements of Catholic doctrine, such as the principles of celibacy and an all-male priesthood, remained largely unaffected by the pressures of religious competition and other contextual influences (see also Iannaccone 1991 and Section 4). It is plausible that this led to sharp differences in Catholics' and Protestants' respective abilities to organize the provision of schooling for girls. In the case of Protestants, the fact that (male) missionaries could marry, and that women sometimes acted as missionaries themselves, implied an important boost to the workforce that could be committed to this task. In many cases, it was the wife of the local pastor who opened the first girls' schools and who subsequently continued to play an active part in running and expanding these facilities (Hastings 1996; Leach 2008). Teaching capacities then usually multiplied after the first female graduates entered the church's local services (Meier zu Selhausen 2014). Catholics, by contrast, were largely deprived of these opportunities. For example, in the case of important mission societies like the White Fathers, female education often had to be "outsourced" to affiliated organizations, such as the White Sisters described above. It is very probable that the resulting institutional divides limited the ability of Catholics to provide schooling for girls at the same scale as Protestants.

Nonetheless, even with these remaining differences in mind, more recent quantitative literature only finds limited evidence about the postulated superior effects of Protestant mission presence on female education. Studies that replace the cross-sectional frameworks of Nunn and Montgomery with cohort-specific analyses of archival and census records usually show that school-related male-to-female differences often tended to *increase* immediately after the arrival of Protestant missionaries (Baten et al. 2021; De Haas and Frankema 2018; Meier zu Selhausen and Weisdorf 2016). Gender imbalances typically only disappeared later in the colonial period, once the state replaced missionaries as the primary provider of education (Baten et al. 2021; De Haas and Frankema 2018; Meier zu Selhausen and Weisdorf 2016). It has been suggested that these results reflect coalescence between missionaries' conservative gender biases and Indigenous patriarchal interests to domesticize women (De Haas and Frankema 2018).

In the remainder of this section, I turn to religious competition as another factor that helps explain limited differences between Catholics and Protestants in the area of female education. The starting assumption of my analysis is the notion that, while differences in religious doctrine and organizational capacities to deliver schooling for girls certainly existed, their effects varied significantly across contexts, depending on the degree of religious competition that existed in a given setting. Although missionaries of both major denominations engaged in female education, it is no exaggeration to argue that for Catholics, these investments primarily reflected a pragmatic response to the practical challenges of winning over new converts. This made their choices in this area much more amendable to the context-specific variation in competitive pressures and strategic considerations outlined above in Section 4. Protestants, by contrast, had both more developed capacities to provide schooling for girls and they assigned more *intrinsic* importance to the question whether converts, including women, were able to read the Bible. Consequently, I expect their behaviors to be less affected by local contexts.

Consistent with my discussion in Section 4 and earlier work by authors like Gallego and Woodberry (2010), the primary variation in my analysis will be introduced by the degree of inter-religious competition permitted by different colonial regimes. As noted, in territories controlled by more interventionist powers like France, Portugal, or Belgium, Catholics often effectively enjoyed a greater degree of protection than Protestants. This reduced the former's incentives to compete for converts on the basis of the quantity and scope of schooling provided. Although Catholic schools certainly existed, and notwithstanding the fact that many of these served girls, the overall scale of female education remained below that offered by Protestants. By contrast, in more competitive religious markets like British colonial Africa, matters were different. The need to compete with Protestants increased incentives for Catholics to invest in schooling as well. This explicitly included the provision of schools for girls. In the overall conservative environment of faith-based female education provision, it was often precisely the opening of these facilities that enabled missions to distinguish themselves from their competitors.

There is historical evidence that these processes indeed played out on the ground. For instance, looking beyond my region of study to the South Indian state of Kerala, Lankina and Getachew (2013) show that the arrival of Protestant missionaries at the onset of British colonial rule upset existing local religious oligopolies between Hinduism and the Syrian and Roman Catholic Churches.[42] The resulting rise in religious competition also led Catholics and the Syrian Church to increase their investments in mass education. This included in particular schooling for girls and other previously underserved groups.

Other evidence of more anecdotal nature also exists from Africa. Numerous reports point to extensive Catholic investments in education in British colonies like Malawi, Nigeria, and Uganda (Boahen 1989; Good 1991; Okonkwo and Ezeh 2008). This also extended to the area of female education. For example, Okonkwo and Ezeh (2008) describe the opening of bespoke girls' schools by French Catholic Sisters in Nigeria as early as the late nineteenth century. Further

---

[42] The latter two existed in Kerala since the days of Thomas the Apostle and sixteenth-century Portuguese conquests, respectively.

south, the Sisters of the Holy Family established convents with primary and boarding schools in the Natal and Orange Free State in 1877 (Boahen 1989). Hodgson (2005) discusses the considerable impact of Catholic missionaries of the Congregation of the Holy Spirit on female education among the Maasai in East Africa. Catholics further acted as innovators in the area of secondary education, which will be the focus of my empirical analysis below. Gallego and Woodberry (2010) note for Malawi and Nigeria that Catholic organizations like the White Fathers were often the first to establish secondary schools, prompting Protestants to follow suit.[43] In Madagascar before the onset of French colonial rule, Jesuits arrived with the intention of opening a high school for girls. They were only discouraged to do so after Protestants lobbied the local Merina Empire to prohibit this innovation (Rabeson 2017).

6.2 Empirical Analysis

The following paragraphs move from anecdotal evidence to more systematic analysis. My starting point is the econometric specification first introduced by Nathan Nunn (2014) in his aforementioned study of the impacts of Catholic and Protestant missions on gender-specific educational attainments. Nunn combines information on historical mission activity from Roome's map with data on contemporary educational attainments from the Afrobarometer surveys. While he reports effects at locality and ethnic group level, I present only locality-specific estimates to circumvent concerns about the reliability of information about early colonial-era ethnic settlement areas (Montgomery 2017). In Nunn's analysis, the locality-specific estimates also produced the clearest Catholic-Protestant gaps in female education, making this a more conservative benchmark for my claim that that the effects of denominational differences were context dependent. A similar research design was subsequently used by Montgomery (2017) for the particular case of present-day Tanzania. The regression specification takes the following form:

$$Education_{ij} = \beta_1 + \beta_2 Protestant_j + \beta_3 Catholic_j + \beta_4\, female_i + \beta_5 Protestant_j \cdot female_i + \beta_6 Catholic_j \cdot female_i + \beta_7 Controls_{ij} + \delta_c + \varepsilon_{ij}$$

Where i identifies the individual survey respondent and j her place of residence (i.e. the survey enumeration area). The first two regressors of primary interest are *Protestant* and *Catholic*. These, respectively, denote the number of

---

[43] In contrast to Protestants' teaching in the local vernacular, Catholics also experimented early with English-language instruction. This created strong competition for Protestants, once the local population recognized English as a more attractive option in the context of the emerging new colonial economy (Gallego and Woodberry 2010).

Protestant and Catholic missions within a 25 km radius of the geographic location of the survey enumeration area. Like Nunn, I draw on Roome's map to identify these missions. *Female,* is a binary indicator that takes the value of 1 if the respondent is a woman. Further iterations below will combine these three variables into different sets of interaction terms. Again following Nunn's earlier approach, I am particularly interested in interactions between *female* and, respectively, *Protestant* and *Catholic*. The latter allow capturing denomination-specific influence of Protestant and Catholic missions on female educational attainments. For instance, a negative and statistically significant coefficient on the interaction of *female* and *Catholic* would indicate relatively lower educational attainments of women in former Catholic mission areas.

The dependent variable (*Education*) is a dummy that takes the value of 1 if a respondent has completed at least secondary education. This is more likely to pick up relevant variation in school attainments in most contemporary African societies, where primary education is now relatively widely accessible to the population. It also helps distinguish potential long-run effects of missionary schools from those of colonial government educational systems, which typically only provided limited secondary education outside of urban areas. A little over 16.800 respondents – or roughly a third of the sample – have completed secondary school. I use a probit model to account for the binary nature of the dependent variable.

6.2.1 Introducing Colonial Regime Contexts

The primary difference where I move beyond Nunn's original research design is the stronger attention to colonial regimes and the varying degrees of inter-missionary competition they allowed. In particular, while Nunn runs his estimations on a pooled sample of eighteen countries, I expand the analysis to a much larger (and historically more diverse) set of thirty-six African nations.[44] This larger sample allows incorporating differences in colonial histories as an additional explanatory dimension. Below I do so primarily through subsample regressions that are divided according to the locally dominant colonial regime type.

Building on previously cited comparativist literature on colonial education systems and the aforementioned article by Gallego and Woodberry (2010), I distinguish between three types of colonial regimes. British colonies are treated as the system that resembled most closely the notion of a competitive

---

[44] I do so by moving from the third round of the Afrobarometer surveys that was used by Nunn to the more expansive sixth wave of the surveys. The countries included in my analysis are Algeria, Benin, Botswana, Burkina Faso, Burundi, Cameroon, Cape Verde, Cote d'Ivoire, Egypt, Gabon, Ghana, Guinea, Kenya, Lesotho, Liberia, Madagascar, Malawi, Mali, Mauritius, Morocco, Mozambique, Namibia, Niger, Nigeria, Sao Tomé and Príncipe; Senegal, Sierra Leone, South Africa, Sudan, Swaziland, Tanzania, Togo, Tunisia, Uganda, Zambia, Zimbabwe.

religious market. As noted, the British not only adopted a relatively liberal approach to the regulation of religious activity. They also largely left it to missionaries to organize the supply of education (Sections 2, 4). The sole constraining factors were restrictions on missionary activity in predominantly Muslim areas (Groves 1969), as well as government grants, which were introduced to encourage minimum quality standards in religious schools (White 1996). British authorities only began monitoring and regulating nonstate providers more actively toward the end of the colonial period, in order to improve the coordination of mission schools with increased public educational investments (Baten et al. 2021; De Haas and Frankema 2018; Jennings 2013).

French colonies are treated here as regimes that permitted much lower levels of competition between Catholics and Protestants.[45] Although most French administrators were staunch laics who did not want to meddle in religious affairs, the majority of them regarded missionaries and their schools with deep suspicion. To them, mission-based education was either of too limited quality or too concerned with religious matters to be of much help in their effort to assimilate Africans into French culture (Rosnes 2017). Consequently, French authorities began to reduce the share of missionary schooling from the first years of colonial rule. In most Francophone colonies, public education systems were introduced soon after the arrival of the colonizers (Huillery 2009; White 1996).[46]

Notwithstanding their strong laicism, French colonizers also afforded Catholics with a range of indirect forms of protection. As noted in Section 4, colonial administrators frequently distrusted the loyalty of "foreign" missions that were active in their territories from the time before the colonial partitioning. The result were policies that proved highly disruptive to Protestants' work. For example, Anglicans were often forced to transfer their vast networks of churches and religious schools to French Protestant missions (Zorn 2012). French missions were also advantaged indirectly, through the requirement that instruction in all schools had to be in French (Clignet and Foster 1964). This new stipulation was easier to fulfill for French Catholics like the White Fathers than for foreign and native Protestant staff who were used to teaching in the local vernacular (see e.g. Rosnes 2017).

---

[45] Somewhat surprisingly, previously cited work by Gallego and Woodberry (2010) treats French-Africa as a region with equally high levels of religious competition as British colonies. This is contradicted by the vast comparative literature on colonial education systems, where French authorities usually emerge as much more interventionistic (see Sections 2 and 4).

[46] This involved a dual structure, with more basic and partially vocational schools for the rural population, and a smaller number of academically more selective lycées and colleges in urban areas (Clignet and Foster 1964; White 1996).

The set of other regime types with more interventionist educational and religious policies is smaller in my sample, due to limitations in the country coverage of the Afrobarometer surveys. I focus here on former Portuguese territories, as a case where Catholics enjoyed particularly strong historical advantages. In regions that were under direct Portuguese control from the fifteenth century, Catholics initially enjoyed a quasi-monopolistic position (Mkenda 2016; Sundkler and Steed 2000). Moreover, like France, Portugal imposed relatively strict language and quality criteria that favored Catholic missions from the home country (Feldmann 2016; Gallego and Woodberry 2010).

I combine Portuguese with former German colonies (pre-1914) into a single category to deal with the small number of non-British and non-French territories in the sample. Although not a predominantly Catholic country, Germany also practiced a highly interventionist approach. For instance, many German missions were created with the explicit purpose of proselytizing and providing education in German colonies (Groves 1969; Hastings 1996). Missions also received government subsidies and cooperated closely with secular authorities in the creation of a local school network (Montgomery 2017). The previously cited study of present-day Tanzania by Montgomery (2017) suggests that these more regulated educational markets resulted in the expected lower levels of female school provision by Catholics. Baten et al.'s (2021) cohort-specific analysis similarly finds large gender gaps among census respondents who were in the schooling age during the German occupation of Tanzania and Cameroon. These inequalities only decreased after the transfer to British and French rule, possibly reflecting higher government investments under the post–World War I League of Nation mandate (Baten et al. 2021).

The regression model also controls for a host of other factors that may predict educational outcomes in their own right. At individual level, these include a binary indicator for Muslim respondents, given that the supply of colonial and mission schooling was much lower for this group, as well as age, and age squared. I also incorporate several indicators of a locality's degree of urbanization and economic development, which are typical correlates of secondary school availability in African countries. These include an identifier for respondents living in urban locations, a measure of road accessibility (average travel time to nearest urban center), population, nighttime light emissions, local infrastructure endowments (water and sanitation supply, health clinics, market stalls, and police and postal offices), distance to the capital and nearest national border, and the share of agricultural and barren land. Finally, I control for a range of geographic and historical variables that emerged as important predictors of local mission presence in earlier literature and in my own analysis in Section 5. These include population sizes in 1900, proximity of an explorer route and colonial railway, distance to the coast, exposure of the locally dominant ethnic group to the slave trade, as well as climatic conditions (temperatures and droughts). All independent variables (except dummies) have been standardized to make comparisons of effect sizes easier and deal with implausibly large coefficients on some of the controls.[47] Effects of a change on the independent variable should therefore be interpreted in terms of standard deviations, not the original measures of the predictors.

Finally, following Nunn's original speciation, I include country fixed effects (δ_c). In the colonizer-specific subsample regressions these will capture historical and contemporary country-specific influences *within* the three colonial regime types described above. I further use two-way clustered standard errors to account for possible correlations between observations within countries and survey enumeration areas.

6.2.2 Results

I begin with the coefficients of *Protestant* and *Catholic*, which provide simple summary measures of the effect of missions of either denomination on the combined educational outcomes of men and women (Table 4, Panel A). *Both* have a significant and positive influence in the full sample (Column 1). This underscores that also Catholics often-made strong contributions to implanting modern education across Africa. Moreover, while the effect is larger for *Protestant,* this difference diminishes in the following estimates (Columns, 2, 4, and 5, respectively). All of the results further indicate a considerable degree of gender inequality in secondary education in the sample. Even controlling for missionary schools, the coefficient for *female* is always large, negative, and highly significant.

Estimates from Column 2 onward include interaction terms between *female* and *Protestant* and *Catholic*, respectively. The model in Column 2 comes closest to Nunn's original specification. It provides gender-differentiated effects of Catholic and Protestant missions for the full sample of countries, without distinguishing between relevant colonial regime contexts. The results broadly support findings reported in Nunn's study (Nunn 2014). In the African average, historical Catholic mission presence is associated with relatively lower female educational attainments today (the coefficient of the interaction term between *female* and *Catholic* is negative and significant). The positive sign of the interaction between *female* and *Protestant* indicates a positive effect of Protestant missionary presence on women's education. Nonetheless, in contrast

---

[47] Significance levels were the same in linear, semi-log and log-in-log regressions.

Table 4 Determinants of secondary school attainments

	(1)	(2)	(3)	(4)	(5)
	Full sample, no interaction	Full sample, with interaction	British colonies	French colonies	Portuguese/ German colonies
	Panel A – Effects of mission presence				
Catholic	**0.030****	**0.049*****	0.031	**0.062*****	**0.055*****
	(0.013)	**(0.018)**	(0.022)	**(0.021)**	**(0.019)**
Protestant	**0.043*****	**0.035*****	**0.043****	0.019	−0.025
	(0.010)	**(0.012)**	**(0.017)**	(0.042)	(0.029)
Female	**−0.311*****	**−0.311*****	**−0.297*****	**−0.371*****	**−0.254*****
	(0.033)	**(0.032)**	**(0.044)**	**(0.059)**	**(0.075)**
Female × Catholic		**−0.039****	−0.022	**−0.098****	**−0.073****
		(0.018)	(0.020)	**(0.039)**	**(0.036)**
Female × Protestant		0.015	−0.005	**0.139****	0.029
		(0.012)	(0.011)	**(0.061)**	(0.029)
Pseudo *R*-squared	0.206	0.207	0.187	0.215	0.154
Observations	49,830	49,830	26,189	14,314	9,327
	Panel B – Effects of Protestant high schools and boarding schools (female sample only)				
Mission boarding/ high schools	**0.042*****		**0.046*****	**0.022*****	0.035
	(0.008)		**(0.016)**	**(0.007)**	(0.022)

Table 4 (cont.)

	(1)	(2)	(3)	(4)	(5)
Panel C – Interaction between Protestant high/boarding schools and female teaching staff (female sample only)					
Mission boarding/high schools		**0.045***	**0.050***	**−1.749**	**0.034***
		(0.011)	**(0.020)**	**(0.685)**	**(0.021)**
Female teaching staff		−0.008	0.000	**0.311***	**−0.105***
		(0.012)	(0.009)	**(0.122)**	**(0.021)**
Interaction		0.000	−0.001	**0.523***	0.060
		(0.003)	(0.002)	**(0.208)**	(0.140)
Panel D – Interaction between Protestant high/boarding schools and male teaching staff (female sample only)					
Mission boarding/ high schools		**0.043***	**0.050***	**1.322***	**0.030***
		(0.009)	**(0.018)**	**(0.337)**	**(0.011)**
Male teaching staff		−0.001	0.031	**−0.201***	**−0.625***
		(0.010)	(0.022)	**(0.052)**	**(0.187)**
Interaction		−0.001	**−0.009***	**−1.600***	**0.136***
		(0.003)	**(0.005)**	**(0.414)**	**(0.028)**

Coefficients from probit estimates. Constant term not reported. See main text for a description of controls and other regression specifications. Standard errors account for clustering at the country and enumeration area level and are reported in parenthesis. ***$p < 0.01$, **$p < 0.05$, *$p < 0.1$

Statistically significant coefficients for key explanatory variables are in bold typeface.

to Nunn's original findings from a smaller study sample, this estimate does not pass the commonly accepted significance thresholds.

Columns 3–5 introduce the role of colonial contexts, based on subsample estimates for the three regime types described above. Overall, these estimates lend strong support to the argument that the degree of religious competition that was permitted by foreign powers had a significant effect on missionary behaviors. Results for British-Africa (Column 3) are consistent with the hypothesis that a less-regulated religious market reduced the effect of denominational differences in female schooling. In this subsample, the coefficient of the interaction between *Catholic* and *female* is small and statistically insignificant.

Of all the subsamples, former French colonies have the highest level of gender inequality in secondary education (Column 5, dummy for *female*). A possible explanation is the fact that French colonial public school systems tended to prioritize investments in higher education among a relatively small, male-dominated elite that was intended to serve in the colonial administration (Baten et al. 2021; Cogneau and Moradi 2014; White 1996). Nonetheless, even in this context, local Catholic mission presence is still associated with a visible educational disadvantage for women. The coefficient of the interaction between *Catholic* and *female* is negative and significant. By comparison, Protestants emerge as a strong compensating influence on gender inequalities. Female educational attainments are significantly higher in localities that had more Protestant missions.

Comparable trends apply to Portuguese and German colonies. The negative effect of Catholic presence on female education is smaller, but still significant (Column 5). This result aligns with that of Montgomery (2017), who documents a similar negative association between Catholic mission presence and female schooling in the specific case of former German East Africa. The influence of Protestant missions on female educational attainments is positive but not statistically distinguishable from zero in this part of the sample.

Estimates in Panels B–D explore possible mechanisms behind the above effects (I report results only for the subsample of female survey respondents to avoid the use of more complex three-way interactions that would otherwise be required for some of the specifications included in the table). Panel B seeks support for the claim that differences in female education are indeed driven by historical variation in mission school supply and not some other channel. *Protestant* is now replaced by the number of Protestant boarding and high schools as the closest equivalent to the contemporary secondary educational outcomes measured by the dependent variable in the above regressions. The data are from Beach's 1903 Atlas that was used to construct Figure 1 in

Section 2.[48] The atlas captures fewer mission stations but it has the advantage that it offers detailed information about the type of services and facilities attached to them. Unfortunately, it does not report data for Catholic missions. Consequently, the following analyses provide partial tests of my arguments for the Protestant subset of missions only.

The results indicate a high degree of persistence in secondary education. The presence of missionary boarding and high schools has a strong and significant influence on contemporary female secondary school attainments. Moreover, this finding now also holds in the subsample of former British colonies. Indeed, the only time where this variable does not have a significant effect is in the smaller and more diverse subsample of former Portuguese and German colonies. However, also here, the coefficient passes the 10 percent threshold once the control for Catholic missions is excluded (not reported).

Beach's atlas does not include information about mission schools that specifically targeted girls. Nonetheless, it has data on the number of female and male teaching staff, which was identified above as a possible reason why Protestants were able to provide higher levels of female education. Here, I interact these variables with the number of missionary boarding and high schools on the assumption that, under the prevailing gender norms of the time, female teachers were more likely to instruct girls (see e.g. Leach 2008). The coefficient of the interaction term indicates that a larger number of female teaching staff in boarding and high schools has a positive influence on women's educational attainments in former French colonies (Panel C). It is worth recalling that this was the only part of the sample where Protestant missions had a significant positive association with contemporary female education in Panel A. Missionaries' historical school provision for girls thus emerges as a plausible transmission mechanism behind this earlier finding. By contrast, the interaction with male teaching staff has a negative influence on female educational attainments in former French and also British colonies (Panel D). Somewhat surprisingly, the interaction has a positive effect in the subsample of former Portuguese and German colonies. However, the noninteracted term for male teaching staff emerges with a very strong negative coefficient.

Other robustness tests in the Element's Annex address the often-noted possibility that trends in long-run gender inequalities in education are really driven by *government* school investments, rather than missionary interventions (see e.g. Baten et al. 2021; De Haas and Frankema 2018). To do so, I control for contemporary public school availability. This does not alter my findings in any significant way.

---

[48] I use Cage and Rueda's (2016) digitized version of the atlas. All variables from the atlas are further weighted by the size of the population in the vicinity of a mission station.

Further tests discount the possibility that missionary presence shaped gender inequalities through other channels than religious school supply. For example, other critical indicators of mission station quality, such as the number of churches, chapels and health facilities typically have smaller and less consistent effects on female educational attainments. Following robustness tests originally applied by Nunn, I also rule out transmission through mission-induced changes in religious attitudes and gender norms. Finally, a set of fixed-effects regressions reveals no other unobserved social or cultural influences operating at the level of subnational regions and ethnic groups.

6.3 Summary and Conclusion

This section has contrasted the predictions of market theory with those of often-made culturalist arguments that highlight deeper-lying doctrinal differences in the educational approaches of Protestant and Catholic missions. My findings suggest that, in the specific case of girls' schooling, these latter claims only apply with important qualifications. In particular in settings with stronger inter-missionary competition, the practical challenges of attracting new converts often offset otherwise more conservative Catholic attitudes toward female education. These results not only support my and other authors' claims that differences in Catholic and Protestant doctrine often did not produce significantly divergence in missionary behaviors on the ground. They also raise wider questions about the emphasis on matters of culture and religious doctrine in the recent literature on mission impacts. My analysis suggests that strategic incentives introduced by different institutional and policy contexts often influenced missionary behaviors in ways that offset deeper-held theological and normative beliefs.

7 Conclusion and Areas for Future Research

This Element engaged with a recent literature in economics and political science that attempts to isolate and quantify the impacts of missionary activity in Africa. It argued that, while this research contributed to more accurate and rigorous assessments of the "true" effects of missionary presence, it also introduced new problems. Often there has been a tendency to present Christian involvement as a largely mechanical and – surprisingly – ahistorical process, that was relatively unaffected by rapidly evolving social, geopolitical, and institutional contexts before and during the colonial annexation of Africa.

Countering this trend, I have illustrated how strongly missionary work was shaped by the particular historical and political environment of Africa around the dawn of the colonial period. In the analyses presented in the last two sections, this was visible especially in the interaction between colonial regimes and the often-intense rivalry between Protestants and Catholics. Both factors had profound implications for the distribution of proselytizing activity and missionaries' strategic choices in important areas like female education. Throughout, my discussion drew strongly on the metaphor of a pluralistic religious market. This builds on a long tradition of sociological and economic thought on the behavior of religious organizations (see e.g. Berger 1969; Iannaccone 1991; Warner 1993). However, somewhat surprisingly, it has been largely absent in the recent interdisciplinary literature on mission studies, following the latter's turn toward questions of culture and religious doctrine (Michalopoulos and Papaioannou 2020; Nunn 2010, 2014).

I conclude with a brief overview of the developments that followed the historical period of missionary activity analyzed here, as well as possible directions for future research that result from them. My discussion focused on the initial phases of the missionary scramble for Africa and its continuation in the first decades of colonial rule. As shown, this period is important for understanding the foundations of strategic choices and spatial and organizational patterns in the subsequent rapid expansion of mission Christianity up to the early twentieth century. However, it omits important changes that set in in later years. In particular the rapid growth of Indigenous Christian movements and so-called African Independent Churches (AICs) deserves mentioning (Horton 1971; Ranger 1986). The latter emerged from the interwar period onward and soon accounted for significant shares of Christians in the region. Many of these new organizations originated from within mainline mission churches and broadly remained within established denominational categories. Nonetheless, they tended to reinforce difference between foreign and African-led forms of organized religious behavior as the new dividing line. Especially AICs were closely associated with anticolonial movements and the "zeitgeist" of African cultural self-determination (Sperber 2017, 16), putting pressure on foreign-dominated mission organizations to allow for a stronger integration of local converts and traditions as well. From the late colonial period onward, they became the main competitors for mainline churches (Ranger 1986; Sperber 2017).

The changing constellation created by the surge in AICs triggered several new dynamics that point to fruitful topics for future investigation under the market-based theory endorsed in this Element. The first noteworthy transformation was the growing shift toward greater collaboration between Catholics and Protestants under the umbrella of the dawning international ecumenical movement of the post-War period. Critical dates were the creation of the Protestant World Council of Churches in 1948 and – on the Catholic side – the Second

Vatican Council from 1962 onward. These initiatives helped overcome the sharp antagonisms between Protestants and Catholics that were identified in Section 4 as one of the primary dividing lines underpinning missionary behavior in previous periods.[49] Exploring how the competition of African-dominated churches contributed to these shifts is a worthy field of investigation. It would also extend the application of market theory beyond more widely studied questions, such as the determinants of missionary education provision discussed in the last section of this Element.

Another area for further research concerns the effects of the historical dynamics outlined here on the relation between religious and secular institutions. Observers of African societies are often struck by how strongly religious beliefs and practices permeate all aspects of social, political, and economic life in the region. This is despite the fact that religion often takes a backseat to other socially or politically more salient identities, such as ethnicity or even class (Ellis and ter Haar 2004; Grossman 2015; McCauley 2017; Sperber 2017).[50] The historical events discussed here and in previous sections of this Element can help illuminate the origins of these developments. For instance, the qualitative evidence discussed in Section 2 suggests that reasons for blurred divides between secular and religious institutions in African societies may be traceable to the early days of 19th-century missionary activity in Africa. In many cases, missionaries' profound spiritualism clashed with the modernizing and secularizing processes of colonial states. The rise of AICs likewise is widely regarded as a contributing factor. Many observers view it as the origin of the dramatic growth of various Pentecostal and nonmainline religious movements that now represent important influences on spiritual and political affairs in contemporary African societies (Ellis and ter Haar 2004; Grossman 2015; McClendon and Riedl 2019; Sperber 2017).

Studying how the above developments in religious practice and relations unfolded is of interest in its own right. In addition, it provides important opportunities to revisit the influence of political regimes on organized religious behaviors. The transition to self-rule was obviously not just shaped by the emergence of new African-led churches, but also by fundamental changes in the structure of government. A particularly relevant question in this context is how independence, as well as the often-highly interventionist and authoritarian

---

[49] Other important changes include the rapid increase in the number of Africans in leading positions of mainline churches and 19th-century growing openness toward the incorporation of local "traditional" beliefs like spirit possession or ancestor worship (McClendon and Riedl 2019; Sperber 2017, 17).

[50] In these settings, attention often moves to specific factors that connect religion to political behavior, such as local political constellations or the content of sermons offered in church (Grossman 2015; McCauley 2017; McClendon and Riedl 2019).

regimes of the 1960s and 70s that followed it, affected new manifestations of religious pluralism, such as the rise of Pentecostalism and other nonmainline churches described above (Ranger 1986; Wright 1971). Analysis of regime influences in this period would also create an important historical link between the discussion of colonial-era missionary work discussed in this Element and an emergent small literature in political science that explores relations between political regimes and religious activity during and after the transition to multiparty states in the 1990s (McCauley 2017; McClendon and Riedl 2019; Riedl 2017; Sperber 2017).

Last but not least, more in-depth analysis of the changes of the late colonial and postindependence period should help illuminate the institutional side of the transmission of educational and other socioeconomic effects of missionary work discussed at multiple points in this Element. For instance, self-rule and the often-attempted nationalization of nonstate services naturally impacted the provision of public goods like education through mainline churches (McClendon and Riedl 2019). Nonetheless, many former missionary organizations held on to their service networks and subsequently became critical pillars of the developmental discourse and voluntary sectors of postcolonial societies (Jennings 2013). These historical continuities are now regarded as an important topic of research in their own right, as they help understand persistence in differences in socioeconomic wellbeing and nonstate service provision in Africa and other developing regions (Jennings 2013; Wietzke 2014; Woodberry 2004, 2012). The market theory endorsed in this Element should again provide additional insights in this context, such as by illuminating how changing regime contexts and new forms of religious competition influenced the behavior of mainline churches and other faith-based organizations in these areas of development.

References

Abernethey, David B. 2000. *The Dynamics of Global Dominance: European Overseas Empires, 1415–1980*. New Haven: Yale University Press.

Acemoglu, Daron, Simon Johnson, and James A. Robinson. 2002. "Reversal of Fortune: Geography and Institutions in the Making of the Modern World Income Distribution." *The Quarterly Journal of Economics* 117(4): 1231–94.

Ajayi, J. F. Ade. 1965. *Christian Missions in Nigeria, 1841–1891*. London: Longman.

Ajayi, J. F. Ade, and Michael Crowder. 1985. *Historical Atlas of Africa*. Harlow: Longman.

Alesina, Alberto, Sebastian Hohmann, Stelios Michalopoulos, and Elias Papaioannou. 2021. "Intergenerational Mobility in Africa." *Econometrica* 89(1): 1–35.

Amasyali, Emre. 2022. "Indigenous Responses to Protestant Missionaries: Educational Competition and Economic Development in Ottoman Turkey." *European Journal of Sociology* 63(1): 39–86.

Austin, Gareth. 2004. *Markets with, without, and in Spite of States: West Africa in the Pre-Colonial Nineteenth Century*. London: Department of Economic History, London School of Economics.

Ayandele, Emmanuel Ayankanmi. 1966. *The Missionary Impact on Modern Nigeria, 1842–1914*. London: Longman.

Balthazar, Joseph, and Michel Kieffer. 1985. "Bishop Francis Xavier Vogt, (1870–1943): A True Disciple of Father Libermann." *Spiritan Papers* 19: 31–47.

Barro, Robert J., and Rachel M. McCleary. 2005. "Which Countries Have State Religions?" *The Quarterly Journal of Economics* 120(4): 1331–70.

Barthel, Diane. 1985. "Women's Educational Experience under Colonialism: Toward a Diachronic Model." *Signs* 11(1): 137–54.

Bastian, Misty L. 2000. "Young Converts: Christian Missions, Gender and Youth in Onitsha, Nigeria 1880–1929." *Anthropological Quarterly* 73(3): 145–58.

Baten, Joerg, Michiel de Haas, Elisabeth Kempter, and Felix Meier zu Selhausen. 2021. "Educational Gender Inequality in Sub-Saharan Africa: A Long-Term Perspective." *Population and Development Review* 47(3): 813–49.

Beach, Harlan P. 1903. *A Geography and Atlas of Protestant Missions: Their Environment, Forces, Distribution, Methods, Problems, Results and*

Prospects at the Opening of the Twentieth Century. Vol II. New York: Student Volunteer Movement for Foreign Missions.

Becker, Sascha O., and Ludger Woessmann. 2008. "Luther and the Girls: Religious Denomination and the Female Education Gap in Nineteenth-Century Prussia." *The Scandinavian Journal of Economics* 110(4): 777–805.

2009. "Was Weber Wrong? A Human Capital Theory of Protestant Economic History." *The Quarterly Journal of Economics* 124(2): 531–96.

Beidelman, Thomas O. 1974. "Social Theory and the Study of Christian Missions in Africa." *Africa: Journal of the International African Institute* 44(3): 235–49.

Berger, Peter L. 1963. "A Market Model for the Analysis of Ecumenicity." *Social Research* 30(1): 77–93.

1969. *The Social Reality of Religion*. London: Faber.

Berman, Edward H. 1974. "African Responses to Christian Mission Education." *African Studies Review* 17(3): 527–40.

Boahen, Adu A. 1989. "New Trends and Processes in Africa in the Nineteenth Century." In *General History of Africa,* Volume VI: *Africa in the Nineteenth Century until the 1880s*, ed. J. F. Ade Ajayi. Paris: UNESCO, 40–63.

Bolt, Jutta, and Dirk Bezemer. 2009. "Understanding Long-Run African Growth: Colonial Institutions or Colonial Education?" *Journal of Development Studies* 45(1): 24–54.

Cage, Julia, and Valeria Rueda. 2016. "The Long-Term Effects of the Printing Press in Sub-Saharan Africa." *American Economic Journal-Applied Economics* 8(3): 69–99.

2020. "Sex and the Mission: The Conflicting Effects of Early Christian Missions on HIV in Sub-Saharan Africa." *Journal of Demographic Economics* 86(3): 213–57.

Caicedo, Felipe Valencia. 2018. "The Mission: Human Capital Transmission, Economic Persistence, and Culture in South America." *The Quarterly Journal of Economics* 134(1): 507–56.

Chesnut, Andrew. 2003. *Competitive Spirits: Latin America's New Religious Economy*. New York: Oxford University Press.

Clignet, Remi P., and Philip J. Foster. 1964. "French and British Colonial Education in Africa." *Comparative Education Review* 8(2): 191–98.

Cogneau, Denis, and Alexander Moradi. 2014. "Borders that Divide: Education and Religion in Ghana and Togo since Colonial Times." *The Journal of Economic History* 74(3): 694–729.

Comaroff, Jean, and John Comaroff. 1993. *Modernity and Its Malcontents: Ritual and Power in Postcolonial Africa*. Chicago, IL: University of Chicago Press.

Comaroff, John, and Jean Comaroff. 2021. "The Colonization of Consciousness." In *Critical Readings in the History of Christian Mission*, Volume 2, ed. Martha Frederiks and Dorottya Nagy. Leiden: Brill, 447–68.

De Haas, Michiel, and Ewout Frankema. 2018. "Gender, Ethnicity, and Unequal Opportunity in Colonial Uganda: European Influences, African Realities, and the Pitfalls of Parish Register Data." *The Economic History Review* 71(3): 965–94.

Depetris-Chauvin, Emilio, and David N. Weil. 2018. "Malaria and Early African Development: Evidence from the Sickle Cell Trait." *The Economic Journal* 128(610): 1207–34.

Donaldson, Dave, and Adam Storeygard. 2016. "The View from Above: Applications of Satellite Data in Economics." *Journal of Economic Perspectives* 30(4): 171–98.

Dupraz, Yannick. 2019. "French and British Colonial Legacies in Education: Evidence from the Partition of Cameroon." *The Journal of Economic History* 79(3): 628–68.

Easton, David. 1959. "Political Anthropology." *Biennial Review of Anthropology* 1: 210–62.

Ellis, Stephen, and Gerrie ter Haar. 2004. *Worlds of Power: Religious Thought and Political Practice in Africa*. Oxford: Oxford University Press.

Feldmann, Horst. 2016. "The Long Shadows of Spanish and French Colonial Education." *Kyklos* 69(1): 32–64.

Finke, Roger, and Rodney Stark. 1988. "Religious Economies and Sacred Canopies: Religious Mobilization in American Cities, 1906." *American Sociological Review* 53(1): 41–49.

Fortes, Meyer, and Edward Evan Evans-Pritchard. 1940. *African Political Systems*. London: Oxford University Press for the International African Institute.

Frankema, Ewout. 2012. "The Origins of Formal Education in Sub-Saharan Africa: Was British Rule More Benign?" *European Review of Economic History* 16(4): 335–55.

Frederiks, Martha, and Dorottya Nagy. 2021. *Critical Readings in the History of Christian Mission*, Volume 2. Leiden: Brill.

Gallego, Francisco A., and Robert Woodberry. 2010. "Christian Missionaries and Education in Former African Colonies: How Competition Mattered." *Journal of African Economies* 19(3): 294–329.

Gauthier, François, and Tuomas Martikainen. 2018. "Introduction: The Marketization of Religion." *Religion* 48(3): 361–66.

Githige, Renison Muchiri. 1982. "The Mission State Relationship in Colonial Kenya: A Summary." *Journal of Religion in Africa* 13(2): 110–25.

Good, Charles M. 1991. "Pioneer Medical Missions in Colonial Africa." *Social Science & Medicine* 32(1): 1–10.

Grier, Robin. 1997. "The Effect of Religion on Economic Development: A Cross National Study of 63 Former Colonies." *Kyklos* 50(1): 47–62.

Grossman, Guy. 2015. "Renewalist Christianity and the Political Saliency of LGBTs: Theory and Evidence from Sub-Saharan Africa." *The Journal of Politics* 77(2): 337–51.

Groves, Charles P. 1969. "Missionary and Humanitarian Aspects of Imperialism from 1870." In *Colonialism in Africa 1870–1960, Volume 1: The History and Politics of Colonialism, 1870–1914*, ed. Lewis H. Gann and Peter Duignan. Cambridge: Cambridge University Press, 462–96.

Guiso, Luigi, Paola Sapienza, and Luigi Zingales. 2006. "Does Culture Affect Economic Outcomes?" *Journal of Economic Perspectives* 20(2): 23–48.

Hastings, Adrian. 1996. *The Church in Africa, 1450–1950*. Oxford: Oxford University Press.

Helmke, Gretchen, and Steven Levitsky. 2004. "Informal Institutions and Comparative Politics: A Research Agenda." *Perspectives on Politics* 2(4): 725–40.

Herbst, Jeffrey Ira. 2000. *States and Power in Africa: Comparative Lessons in Authority and Control*. Princeton, NJ: Princeton University Press.

Hodgson, Dorothy Louise. 2005. *The Church of Women: Gendered Encounters between Maasai and Missionaries*. Bloomington: Indiana University Press.

Horton, Robin. 1971. "African Conversion." *Africa: Journal of the International African Institute* 41(2): 85–108.

Höschele, Stefan. 2010. "From Mission Comity to Interdenominational Relations: The Development of the Adventist Statement on Relationships with Other Christian Churches." In *Exploring the Frontiers of Faith: Festschrift in Honour of Dr. Jan Paulsen*, ed. Borge Schantz and Reinder Bruinsma. Lueneburg: Advent-Verlag, 389–404.

Huillery, Elise. 2009. "History Matters: The Long-Term Impact of Colonial Public Investments in French West Africa." *American Economic Journal: Applied Economics* 1(2): 176–215.

Hunt, Nancy Rose. 1990. "Domesticity and Colonialism in Belgian Africa: Usumbura's Foyer Social, 1946–1960." *Signs* 15(3): 447–74.

Iannaccone, Laurence. 1991. "The Consequences of Religious Market Structure." *Rationality and Society* 3: 156–77.

Jedwab, Remi, Felix Meier zu Selhausen, and Alexander Moradi. 2021. "Christianization without Economic Development: Evidence from

Missions in Ghana." *Journal of Economic Behavior & Organization* 190: 573–96.

2022. "The Economics of Missionary Expansion: Evidence from Africa and Implications for Development." *Journal of Economic Growth* 27(2): 149–92.

Jennings, Michael. 2013. "Common Counsel, Common Policy: Healthcare, Missions and the Rise of the 'Voluntary Sector' in Colonial Tanzania." *Development and Change* 44(4): 939–63.

Johnson, Hildegard Binder. 1967. "The Location of Christian Missions in Africa." *Geographical Review* 57(2): 168–202.

Kitaev, Igor. 1999. *Private Education in Sub-Saharan Africa: A Re-Examination of Theories and Concepts Related to Its Development and Finance.* Paris: UNESCO.

Klein Goldewijk, Kees, Arthur Beusen, Gerard van Drecht, and Martine de Vos. 2011. "The HYDE 3.1 Spatially Explicit Database of Human-Induced Global Land-Use Change Over the Past 12,000 Years." *Global Ecology and Biogeography* 20(1): 73–86.

Landau, Paul Stuart. 1995. *The Realm of the Word: Language, Gender, and Christianity in a Southern African Kingdom.* London: James Currey.

Lankina, Tomila, and Lullit Getachew. 2012. "Mission or Empire, Word or Sword? The Human Capital Legacy in Postcolonial Democratic Development." *American Journal of Political Science* 56(2): 465–83.

2013. "Competitive Religious Entrepreneurs: Christian Missionaries and Female Education in Colonial and Post-Colonial India." *British Journal of Political Science* 43(1): 103–31.

Latourette, Kenneth Scott. 1963. "Ecumenical Beginnings in Protestant World Mission: A History of Comity. By R. Pierce Beaver. New York: Thomas Nelson and Sons, 1962. 356 pp." *Journal of Church and State* 5(1): 113–14.

Leach, Fiona. 2008. "African Girls, Nineteenth-Century Mission Education and the Patriarchal Imperative." *Gender and Education* 20(4): 335–47.

Lloyd, Peter C. 1965. "The Political Structure of African Kingdoms: An Exploratory Model." In *Political Systems and the Distribution of Power*, ed. Michael Banton. London: Routledge, 63–112.

Markowitz, Marvin D. 1973. *Cross and Sword: The Political Role of Christian Missions in the Belgian Congo, 1908–1960.* Stanford, Cal: Hoover Institution Press.

McCauley, John F. 2017. *The Logic of Ethnic and Religious Conflict in Africa.* Cambridge: University of California Press.

McCleary, Rachel M., and Robert J. Barro. 2019. "Protestants and Catholics and Educational Investment in Guatemala." In *Advances in the Economics of*

Religion, ed. Jean-Paul Carvalho, Sriya Iyer, and Jared Rubin. Cham: Springer International, 169–95.

McClendon, Gwyneth H., and Rachel Beatty Riedl. 2019. *From Pews to Politics: Religious Sermons and Political Participation in Africa*. Cambridge, UK: Cambridge University Press.

Meier zu Selhausen, Felix. 2014. "Missionaries and Female Empowerment in Colonial Uganda: New Evidence from Protestant Marriage Registers, 1880–1945." *Economic History of Developing Regions* 29(1): 74–112.

Meier zu Selhausen, Felix, and Jacob Weisdorf. 2016. "A Colonial Legacy of African Gender Inequality? Evidence from Christian Kampala, 1895–2011." *The Economic History Review* 69(1): 229–57.

Michalopoulos, Stelios, and Elias Papaioannou. 2020. "Historical Legacies and African Development." *Journal of Economic Literature* 58(1): 53–128.

Mkenda, Festo. 2016. "Jesuits and Africa." In *Oxford Handbooks Online*. Oxford: Oxford University Press.

2018. "A Protestant Verdict on the Jesuit Missionary Approach in Africa: David Livingstone and Memories of the Early Jesuit Presence in South Central Africa." In *Encounters between Jesuits and Protestants in Africa*, eds. Robert Aleksander Maryks and Festo Mkenda, S.J.. Leiden, NL: Brill, 59–80.

Montgomery, Max. 2017. "Colonial Legacy of Gender Inequality: Christian Missionaries in German East Africa." *Politics & Society* 45(2): 225–68.

Murdock, George Peter. 1967. *Ethnographic Atlas*. Pittsburgh, PA: University of Pittsburgh Press.

Murhula, Toussaint Kafarhire. 2018. "Jesuit–Protestant Encounters in Colonial Congo in the Late Nineteenth Century: Perceptions, Prejudices, and the Competition for African Souls." In *Encounters between Jesuits and Protestants in Africa*, eds. Robert Aleksander Maryks and Festo Mkenda, S.J.. Leiden, NL: Brill, 194–214.

Nikolova, Elena, and Jakub Polansky. 2020. "Conversionary Protestants Do Not Cause Democracy." *British Journal of Political Science* 51(4), 1723–1733.

Nordhaus, William D. 2006. "Geography and Macroeconomics: New Data and New Findings." *Proceedings of the National Academy of Sciences* 103(10): 3510–17.

Nunn, Nathan. 2008. "The Long-Term Effects of Africa's Slave Trades." *The Quarterly Journal of Economics* 123(1): 139–76.

2010. "Religious Conversion in Colonial Africa." *American Economic Review* 100(2): 147–52.

2014. "Gender and Missionary Influence in Colonial Africa." In *Africa's Development in Historical Perspective*, ed. Emmanuel Akyeampong,

Robert Bates, Nathan Nunn, and James A. Robinson. New York: Cambridge University Press, 489–512.

Okonkwo, Uche Uwaezuoke, and Mary-Noelle Ethel Ezeh. 2008. "Implications of Missionary Education for Women in Nigeria: A Historical Analysis." *Journal of International Women's Studies* 10(2): 186–97.

Okoye, Dozie. 2021. "Things Fall Apart? Missions, Institutions, and Interpersonal Trust." *Journal of Development Economics* 148: 102568.

Opoku, K. Asare. 1985. "Religion in Africa during the Colonial Era." In *General History of Africa, Volume 7: Africa under Colonial Domination, 1880–1935*, ed. A. Adu Boahen. Paris: UNESCO, 506–38.

Osterhammel, Juergen. 2014. *The Transformation of the World: A Global History of the Nineteenth Century*. Princeton: Princeton University Press.

Pawliková-Vilhanová, Viera. 2007. "Christian Missions in Africa and Their Role in the Transformation of African Societies." *Asian and African Studies* 16(2): 249–60.

Pfisterer, H. 1933. "Der Wettbewerb Der Katholischen Mit Der Deutschen Evangelischen Mission." *Neue Allgemeine Missionszeitschrift* 10 (2–6).

Pierskalla, Jan, Alexander De Juan, and Max Montgomery. 2019. "The Territorial Expansion of the Colonial State: Evidence from German East Africa 1890–1909." *British Journal of Political Science* 49(2): 711–37.

Porta, Rafael La, Florencio Lopez-de-Silanes, Andrei Shleifer, and Robert W. Vishny. 1997. "Trust in Large Organizations." *The American Economic Review* 87(2): 333–38.

Porter, Andrew. 2004. *Religion versus Empire? British Protestant Missionaries and Overseas Expansion, 1700–1914*. Manchester, UK: Manchester University Press.

Putnam, Robert D. 1993. *Making Democracy Work: Civic Traditions in Modern Italy*. Princeton, NJ: Princeton University Press.

Rabeson, Jocelyn. 2017. "Jesuits and Protestants in Nineteenth-Century Madagascar." In *Encounters between Jesuits and Protestants in Africa*, eds. Maryks, Robert A., and Mkenda, Festo S.J. Leiden, NL: Brill, 169–93.

Ranger, Terence O. 1986. "Religious Movements and Politics in Sub-Saharan Africa." *African Studies Review* 29(2): 1–69.

1999. "'Taking on the Missionary's Task': African Spirituality and the Mission Churches of Manicaland in the 1930s." *Journal of Religion in Africa* 29(2): 175–205.

Riedl, Rachel Beatty. 2017. "Sub-National–Cross-National Variation: Method and Analysis in Sub-Saharan Africa." *American Behavioral Scientist* 61(8): 932–59.

Roberts, A. D. 2008. "Livingstone, David (1813–1873), Explorer and Missionary." *Oxford Dictionary of National Biography*. www.oxforddnb.com/view/10 .1093/ref:odnb/9780198614128.001.0001/odnb-9780198614128-e-16803.

Roome, William. R. M. 1925. *Ethnographic Survey of Africa: Showing the Tribes and Languages; Also the Stations of Missionary Societies*. Edward Stanford Ltd.

Rosnes, Ellen Vea. 2017. "Christianisation, Frenchification and Malgachisation: Mission Education during War and Rebellion in French Colonial Madagascar in the 1940s." *History of Education* 46(6): 747–67.

Smith, Adam. [1776] 1965. *An Inquiry into the Nature and Causes of the Wealth of Nations*. New York: Modern Library.

Smythe, Kathleen R. 2007. "African Women and White Sisters at the Karema Mission Station, 1894–1920." *Journal of Women's History* 19(2): 59–84.

Sperber, Elizabeth Sheridan. 2017. "Deus Ex achina? New Religious Movements in African Politics. Unpublished Doctoral thesis. Columbia University, New York.. Available at: https://academiccommons.columbia. edu/doi/10.7916/D8474B61

Stanley, Brian. 1983. "'Commerce and Christianity': Providence Theory, the Missionary Movement, and the Imperialism of Free Trade, 1842–1860." *The Historical Journal* 26(1): 71–94.

Stanley, Brian. 1990. *The Bible and the Flag: Protestant Missions and British Imperialism in the Nineteenth and Twentieth Centuries*. Leicester, UK: Apollos.

Strayer, Robert. 1976. "Mission History in Africa: New Perspectives on an Encounter." *African Studies Review* 19(1): 1–15.

Sundkler, Bengt, and Christopher Steed. 2000. *A History of the Church in Africa*. Cambridge: Cambridge University Press.

Thornton, John Kelly. 1998. *The Kongolese Saint Anthony: Dona Beatriz Kimpa Vita and the Antonian Movement, 1684–1706*. New York: Cambridge University Press.

Tollefsen, Andreas Forø, Håvard Strand, and Halvard Buhaug. 2012. "PRIO-GRID: A Unified Spatial Data Structure." *Journal of Peace Research* 49(2): 363–74.

Trejo, Guillermo. 2009. "Religious Competition and Ethnic Mobilization in Latin America: Why the Catholic Church Promotes Indigenous Movements in Mexico." *American Political Science Review* 103(3): 323–42.

Waldinger, Maria. 2017. "The Long-Run Effects of Missionary Orders in Mexico." *Journal of Development Economics* 127: 355–78.

Wallerstein, Immanuel. 1961. *Africa: The Politics of Independence*. New York: Vintage Books.

Wantchekon, Leonard, Marko Klašnja, and Natalija Novta. 2015. "Education and Human Capital Externalities: Evidence from Colonial Benin." *Quarterly Journal of Economics* 130(2): 703–57.

Warner, R. Stephen. 1993. "Work in Progress Toward a New Paradigm for the Sociological Study of Religion in the United States." *American Journal of Sociology* 98(5): 1044–93.

White, Bob W. 1996. "Talk about School: Education and the Colonial Project in French and British Africa, (1860–1960)." *Comparative Education* 32(1): 9–25.

Wietzke, Frank-Borge. 2014. "Historical Origins of Uneven Service Supply in Sub-Saharan Africa: The Role of Non-State Providers." *Journal of Development Studies* 50(12): 1614–30.

2015. "Long-Term Consequences of Colonial Institutions and Human Capital Investments: Sub-National Evidence from Madagascar." *World Development* 66: 293–307.

Wodon, Quentin. 2020. "How Well Do Catholic and Other Faith-Based Schools Serve the Poor? A Study with Special Reference to Africa: Part II: Learning." *International Studies in Catholic Education* 12(1): 3–20.

Woodberry, Robert D. 2004. "The Shadow of Empire: Christian Missions, Colonial Policy, and Democracy in Postcolonial Societies." Unpublished Doctoral thesis. University of North Carolina.

2008. "Reclaiming the M-Word: The Legacy of Missions in Nonwestern Societies." *International Journal of Frontier Missiology* 25(1): 17–23.

2011. *Ignoring the Obvious: What Explains Botswana's Exceptional Democratic and Economic Performance in Sub-Saharan Africa*. Project on Religion and Economic Change Working Paper No. 5.

2012. "The Missionary Roots of Liberal Democracy." *American Political Science Review* 106(2): 244–74.

Wright, Marcia. 1971. "African History in the 1960's: Religion." *African Studies Review* 14(3): 439–45.

Young, Crawford. 1994. *The African Colonial State in Comparative Perspective*. New Haven: Yale University Press.

Zorn, Jean-Francois. 2012. "When French Protestants Replaced British Missionaries in the Pacific and Indian Oceans; or, How to Avoid the Colonial Trap." In *In God's Empire: French Missionaries in the Modern World*, ed. J. P. Daughton and Owen White. Oxford: Oxford University Press.

Acknowledgments

Research for this Element was supported by the Spanish Ministry of Economy Industry and Competitiveness (MINECO) through its Academic Excellence and Societal Challenges initiative (grant number CSO2017-87350-P). The bulk of this manuscript was completed during a stay as a Jean-Monnet visiting fellow at the European University Institute (EUI), Florence. I am grateful for comments on earlier drafts by Cathy Boone, Melani Cammett, two anonymous reviewers, seminar participants at the EUI, as well as the series' editors Rachel Riedl and Ben Ross Schneider. Thank you to my father Joachim Wietzke for his comments and help in accessing historical sources from German libraries. As always, I am particularly grateful to my wife Hannah for her unwavering support, patience, and editorial help during the writing process. I would not be able to complete these projects without her.

Cambridge Elements ≡

Politics of Development

Rachel Beatty Riedl

Einaudi Center for International Studies and Cornell University

Rachel Beatty Riedl is the Director and John S. Knight Professor of the Einaudi Center for International Studies and Professor in the Government Department and School of PublicPolicy at Cornell University. Riedl is the author of the award-winning Authoritarian Originsof Democratic Party Systems in Africa (2014) and co-author of From Pews to Politics: Religious Sermons and Political Participation in Africa (with Gwyneth McClendon, 2019).She studies democracy and institutions, governance, authoritarian regime legacies, andreligion and politics in Africa. She serves on the Editorial Committee of World Politics andthe Editorial Board of African Affairs, Comparative Political Studies, Journal of Democracy,and Africa Spectrum. She is co-host of the podcast Ufahamu Africa.

Ben Ross Schneider

Massachusetts Institute of Technology

Ben Ross Schneider is Ford International Professor of Political Science at MIT and Director of the MIT-Brazil program. Prior to moving to MIT in 2008, he taught at Princeton University and Northwestern University. His books include Business Politics and the State in 20th Century Latin America (2004), Hierarchical Capitalism in Latin America (2013), Designing Industrial Policy in Latin America: Business-Government Relations and the NewDevelopmentalism (2015), and New Order and Progress: Democracy and Development in Brazil (2016). He has also written on topics such as economic reform, democratization, education, labor markets, inequality, and business groups.

Advisory Board

Yuen Yuen Ang *University of Michigan*
Catherine Boone *London School of Economics*
Melani Cammett, *Harvard University* (former editor)
Stephan Haggard *University of California, San Diego*
Prerna Singh *Brown University*
Dan Slater *University of Michigan*

About the Series

The Element series *Politics of Development* provides important contributions on both established and new topics on the politics and political economy of developing countries. A particular priority is to give increased visibility to a dynamic and growing body of social science research that examines the political and social determinants of economic development, as well as the effects of different development models on political and social outcomes.

Cambridge Elements ≡

Politics of Development

Elements in the Series

Developmental States
Stephan Haggard

Coercive Distribution
Michael Albertus, Sofia Fenner and Dan Slater

Participation in Social Policy: Public Health in Comparative Perspective
Tulia G. Falleti and Santiago L. Cunial

Undocumented Nationals
Wendy Hunter

Democracy and Population Health
James W. McGuire

Rethinking the Resource Curse
Benjamin Smith and David Waldner

Greed and Guns: Imperial Origins of the Developing World
Atul Kohli

Everyday Choices: The Role of Competing Authorities and Social Institutions in Politics and Development
Ellen M. Lust

Locked Out of Development: Insiders and Outsiders in Arab Capitalism
Steffen Hertog

Power and Conviction: The Political Economy of Missionary Work in Colonial-Era Africa
Frank-Borge Wietzke

A full series listing is available at: www.cambridge.org/EPOD

Printed in the United States
by Baker & Taylor Publisher Services